# SOCIAL A
## MAF

CU00553195

## ⊓⌐ DASICS

*Social and Labour Market Policy: The Basics* is an engaging and accessible introduction to the subject, which explores the broad historical, social and economic factors which have affected the differing types of social and labour market policies found in welfare states. Drawing links between social policy and labour market policy the book explores key introductory topics including:

- Defining what we mean when we speak of social policy and labour market policy
- Historical origins including Bismarckian and Beveridgian reforms
- The range of social issues social policy aims to address, e.g. housing policy and child provision
- Showing how social policy enhances well-being
- Ideas and ideology and the effects of globalisation
- The functioning of the labour market.

*Social and Labour Market Policy: The Basics* provides readers with an understanding of their importance to the development of contemporary society. This book is suitable for students of social policy as well as students taking a social policy module as part of a wider course within politics, social work, health care, sociology and economics. Researchers interested in the field will also benefit from reading this book.

**Bent Greve** is Professor in Social Science with an emphasis on welfare state analysis at the University of Roskilde, Denmark. His research interest focuses on the welfare state, and social and labour market policy, often from a comparative perspective. He has published extensively on social and labour market policy, social security, tax expenditures, public sector expenditures and financing of the welfare state. He is editor of *Social Policy & Administration*. Recent books include *Long-Term Care for the Elderly in Europe: Development and Prospects* (ed., 2017); *Handbook of Social Policy Evaluation* (ed., 2017); *Technology and the Future of Work* (2017); *The Impact on Labour Markets and Welfare States* (2017).

# The Basics

For a full list of titles in this series, please visit www.routledge.com/The-basics/book-series/B

"In this very concise and well-written book, Bent Greve provides a compelling introduction to the closely-related areas of social policy and labour market policy. His short book should help students, researchers, and informed readers to grasp the meaning of key concepts in these two areas."

*—Daniel Béland, Johnson-Shoyama Graduate School of Public Policy, Canada*

"At a time when social and labour market policies are under increasing scrutiny, this lively new book attempts to systematize and critically analyse what is known about these core functions of the modern welfare state. What is 'social' and 'labour market policy', how have these policies evolved, and how do they relate? How do social and labour market policies and functions differ across nations, what are their effects and what societal outcomes do they produce? *Social and Labour Market Policy: The Basics* is an invaluable contribution to understanding the issues and pressing challenges facing welfare systems ahead."

*—Christopher Deeming,* Journal of Social Policy *and University of Strathclyde, UK*

# SOCIAL AND LABOUR MARKET POLICY
## THE BASICS

Bent Greve

LONDON AND NEW YORK

First published 2018
by Routledge
2 Park Square, Milton Park, Abingdon, Oxon OX14 4RN

and by Routledge
711 Third Avenue, New York, NY 10017

*Routledge is an imprint of the Taylor & Francis Group, an informa business*

*British Library Cataloguing-in-Publication Data*
A catalogue record for this book is available from the British Library

*Library of Congress Cataloguing-in-Publication Data*
Names: Greve, Bent, author.
Title: Social and labour market policy : the basics / Bent Greve.
Description: Abingdon, Oxon ; New York, NY : Routledge, 2018. |
    Includes bibliographical references and index.
Identifiers: LCCN 2017045738 | ISBN 9781138557284 (hardback) |
    ISBN 9781138557291 (pbk.) | ISBN 9781315150802 (ebook)
Subjects: LCSH: Social policy. | Labor policy.
Classification: LCC HN18.3 .G74 2018 | DDC 306—dc23
LC record available at https://lccn.loc.gov/2017045738

ISBN: 978-1-138-55728-4 (hbk)
ISBN: 978-1-138-55729-1 (pbk)
ISBN: 978-1-315-15080-2 (ebk)

Typeset in Bembo
by Apex CoVantage, LLC

# CONTENTS

# FIGURES

# TABLES

# FOREWORD

Social and labour market policy is central in everyday modern societies. All welfare states have a plethora of systems, variations in size and ways of implementation, and also a historical legacy.

This is reflected in this book, which attempts to systematise and analyse these two core areas in order not only to inform the reader about the issues, but also to create new insights and knowledge about the systems.

Having only a limited space, this is not a simple task. I hope it has been successful.

While writing the book I have benefitted from updating, revising and editing the 2nd edition of *The Routledge Handbook of the Welfare State*, which has helped me to ensure that this book is up to date and at the front line of what is central in social and labour market policy. Therefore, thanks to the many contributors to that book. As there are several topics in this book for which it has it not been possible to go into detail, I therefore make frequent reference to the *Handbook*.

Naturally, as always in books, the author is responsible for all faults and mistakes.

Bagsværd and Roskilde, September, 2017
Bent Greve

# ABBREVIATIONS

| | |
|---|---|
| ALMP | active labour market policy |
| ESSPROS | European system of integrated social protection statistics |
| EU | European Union, http://europa.eu/european-union/index_en |
| GDP | gross domestic product |
| ILO | International Labour Organization, www.ilo.org/global/lang--en/index.htm |
| IMF | International Monetary Fund, www.imf.org/external/index.htm |
| NGO | non-governmental organisation |
| OECD | Organisation for Economic Co-operation and Development, www.oecd.org/ |
| OMC | open method of coordination |
| PES | public employment services |
| UN | United Nations, www.un.org/en/index.html |
| VAT | value-added tax |
| WHO | World Health Organization, www.who.int/en/ |

# WHAT IS IT ALL ABOUT?

## 1.1. INTRODUCTION

In all societies, there are different kinds of social and labour market policy. Rich societies often have a more developed focus on such policies and have developed what is labelled welfare states. The degree of, approach to and types of welfare financed and delivered by the state – or other actors – varies between countries. This can often be ascribed to historical traditions, ideas and a certain kind of path-dependency. Still, there are many and diverse ways of supporting people with different kinds of needs and in dissimilar social circumstances. These ways have also changed over time because of development in societies, increasingly open societies and new ways of producing goods and services, including fewer jobs in traditional production in the agricultural and industrial sectors.

Furthermore, economic development with, in most cases, societies growing richer has also caused a shift away from nearly all social security being taken care of within families and/or churches and other voluntary organisations, and towards a role for the market and companies. Gradually, there has been a move towards the approach of stronger state influence, or at least some state involvement. State regulation of social and working conditions, such as child labour being made illegal and other types of regulation have gradually developed over time. The interplay between nation states and supranational entities, such as the European Union (EU), has also influenced the development of these issues, and economic and political pressures due to globalisation have also had an impact.

The development of social and labour market policy has not merely happened in a vacuum, but it has been framed by options (political and economic), conflicts and pressure from interest groups for changes. There are thus not only different connotations of what social and labour market policy is, but also many other issues at stake for groups in society with different needs and the willingness to pay for welfare.

Despite this, the concepts are not clear, an issue to be returned to in Section 1.3. This first chapter focuses on what the concepts of social and labour market policy are and how they can be understood. It begins with a short historical depiction of the development, using the lenses of old and new social risk (Taylor-Gooby, 2004) as a way to see how policies have developed. The new social risk can be described as "the risks that people now face in the course of their lives as a result of the economic and social changes associated with the transition to the post-industrial society" (pp. 2–3). The old risk related to the movement from the countryside into the cities, resulting in the need for support when people became unemployed, sick, old and after an industrial injury. Not only does the historical transition influence policies, but also the ongoing changes in society's structure affect the possible need for public support for welfare.

It is also worth emphasising some of the central themes and persons having been influential in the development of the policies, as this to a certain extent helps in understanding the present day's social and labour market policy. This is set out in Section 1.2.

The first chapter ends with a short overview of what to expect in the book.

Overall, the aim of the book is to present and discuss the following issues:

a) What is social and labour market policy?
b) The principles for delivering social and labour market policies

c) Who are the central actors and what is their interest?
d) How do policies differ among different countries – and for what reason?
e) What influences the development?
f) What does and does not work in the field?
g) What is the overall impact on societies' development – including redistribution and level of equality?

This is done by presenting core concepts, discussing and analysing changes in the field, and using existing studies and new data to show what social and labour market policy actually is, and how it has been developing in recent years. It emphasises that a concrete way of implementing policies varies across countries, so that how the system looks in one's own country cannot be used as an indication that this is the way it is in all countries. The focus is on principles, but examples of concrete approaches are given. The presentation of concepts and issues is also interpreted in line with expectations for changing societies in the years to come, such as technology's impact on the number and types of jobs, and the possible implication not only for labour markets, but also in the way social policy can have a role, including difficult issues related to financing welfare in a global technological world.

## 1.2. HISTORICAL TRAJECTORIES

Social and labour market policy as it is today has not just appeared overnight. In most countries, it has in fact developed over a long period, starting with a few areas and gradually moving into broader and more encompassing coverage. Sometimes this development has been along the same path; however, in relation to retrenchment, re-calibration and break-up, the development has sometimes not taken the historical path. Changes are sometimes done in line with the ideological stance of incoming governments, and sometimes as a consequence of external economic circumstances. Changes have also come about as a consequence of new ways of living and new types of social risk. Therefore, even if the historical ways of delivering and financing social and labour market policy are no longer in existence, they tell the story of what the policy is and the reasons why the systems look like they do. Historical development is also framed by the fact that countries today are more affluent than they were in the heyday of the development. Therefore, it has been possible to bring new aspects and elements into what is provided by the welfare state, and also how generous the different welfare states are able to be. This also reflects the increased expectation of citizens (and voters) of the level of benefits and size and quality of services available. This is not so say that cutbacks and austerity measures are not important, as several countries, over time, have witnessed even stronger changes with less spending on welfare policies. This section paints a snapshot of the development by looking into a few central people's ideas and contributions to the historical development, and hereby pointing towards important aspects of the development, and also, implicitly, the central concept. How this is then related to social and labour market policy is more elaborated in Section 1.3.

Although state involvement in social and labour market policy is relatively new, a poor law was enacted in England in 1388, with the aim that local areas should provide support for individuals. It was changed in 1834 to make it more general, and workhouses were established where those in need of support should work. In many countries, poor laws have been the first approach towards social policy, and often with a distinction between those who were seen as deserving compared to the undeserving. Poor laws were later often changed into what we know today as social assistance. A distinction between deserving and undeserving is not often used in public discourse today, but habitually it implicitly lies beneath policy, in the form of those who deserve support are those who have been working hard and are in need of support due to reasons beyond their control; see also Chapter 4. The historical level of support was a long way from what we understand today as generous social policy, and, in most countries, families and churches were central in supporting those in need.

Otto von Bismarck is often labelled as one of the founding fathers of that part of social policy as we know it today. In Prussia in the 1880s, compulsory social insurance schemes in relation to sickness, industrial accidents and old age (e.g. pensions) were established. The development is often argued to be due to, and developed as, a wish to reduce the political pressure in the wake of industrialisation, where families not having in-family support who moved to the cities in order to get a job might in cases of unemployment or industrial injury be without any support, which could lead to social unrest. This way of providing benefits (social insurance), especially for those who are in the labour market, is still today the main element in many countries of the central European social policy. Thus, it emphasises the impact of path-dependency even in today's welfare states, which are often built upon historical decisions. However, this does not imply that it cannot be very different from the way the system is now, which is the case in many countries – regarding who has access to benefits, the conditions to receive benefits, and the level of benefits, etc. compared to historic cases. Still, the social insurance principle has played a strong role in the development of social and labour market policy in many countries.

Another central person is John Maynard Keynes, who has been very influential in economic thinking in relation to his writing, especially in the 1930s. For this book, the central aspect is that government can influence the overall economic development, and by public initiatives influence the general level of employment and unemployment. Roosevelt's New Deal in the United States in 1933 is also an example of the thinking that the use of government intervention, by, for example, building infrastructure such as roads, railroads and harbours could have an impact on the number of people in jobs. The simple idea being that those doing the work would be employed, and when they have money to spend this would increase the demand for goods and services and thereby for others to work in the economy, and in that way influencing the overall economic development; see more in Chapter 5.

Sir William Beveridge is another central name in the development of welfare states, and, as a consequence, what is important in the fields of social and labour market policy, as argued in the report written during the Second World War: "Want is only one of the five giants on the road of reconstruction, and in some ways the easiest to attach. The others are Disease, Ignorance, Squalor and Idleness" (quoted in Timmins, 1995, p. 23). From these five giants were developed the ideas and principles towards the building in the United Kingdom of what we today label the liberal welfare state, but they have also influenced the Nordic welfare states' more universal approach, which – albeit at a later stage – developed in a more generous, encompassing and universalistic direction. Beveridge's ideas included the universal provision of welfare and the ambition of full employment, but also flat-rate means-tested benefits at a low level, financed overall through general taxation. Comprehensive health care and support to children were also included. Overall, it was argued that the welfare system should be built upon three elements. These were: a) social insurance for basic needs, b) national assistance for special cases and c) voluntary insurance for assistance above the basic level.

The golden growth of welfare states (Esping-Andersen, 1996; Esping-Andersen, 1999) is often labelled as the time from around 1960 to the start of the first oil-price crisis. Due to economic growth, increasing prosperity and, in many countries, the possibility of, at the same time, increasing private as well as public consumption, it was argued that this would keep the unemployment rate low and with stable economic development. In this era, it was further common wisdom that societies, by accepting Keynesian intervention, would have an option to steer the economy in such a way that negative repercussions on living standards could be avoided. The working class and trade unions were strong, and tendencies towards more equal societies were on the agenda.

The first and later the second oil-price crisis with a quadrupling of oil prices caused an increase in unemployment and inflation and a stagnation of economic development. This, together with criticism of welfare states for being too bureaucratic, caused a growing discontent with social and labour market policy. Overall, it can be argued that, as it was carried out at that time, policies shifted from overall acceptance of the expansion to criticism, including retrenchment and privatisation (Miller, 1990). Further, the Organisation for Economic Co-operation and Development (OECD) declared the welfare state in crisis (OECD, 1981). This was primarily due to the lack of ability to steer through the crisis with the instruments used earlier, and of entering a time of stagflation, for example low, if any, economic growth and high levels of inflation. This gave rise to a belief in a more liberal or neo-liberal approach, where the state's role in social and labour market policy was questioned, and with a stronger focus and ambition to bring back the market as the central institution in delivering and financing in relation to social and labour market policy.

Whether spending is a burden or whether social policy also has a positive role has come to the fore in several ways in recent years, including Giddens's *Third Way* (1998); see also Morel, Palier and Plame (2012) on social policy as investment, for example, the debate on the social-investment state.

Since then, there have been ongoing discussions on the central aspects related to the policies, such as:

- the size and depth of social and labour market policy (including what can we afford)
- how to implement the policies
- how to ensure the policies are efficient
- how to reach the target groups
- who will have to pay, and in what way
- what the impact of policies is on inequality

These six questions stand as central parameters for the presentation in this book.

These debates are often framed in different ideological positions, but also in how different professions and interest groups see the need to bring their field more into the core of the social and labour market policy; see also Chapter 5.

Voters' support has also varied, dependent on the type of social and labour market policy. This includes the indirect issue of the deserving and the non-deserving; see more in Chapters 2 and 4. Support from voters is part of the legitimacy of welfare states, and, often, high on the list has been support for health care and the elderly.

## 1.3.  WHAT IS SOCIAL AND LABOUR MARKET POLICY?

Overall, social policy can be seen as central policies in welfare states, for example, social security, education, health care and housing. It might even reflect labour market policy, albeit in this book labour market policy is treated separately.

Often, social policy is, at the central level, taken care of in a ministry of social security, but has different names in different countries (social policy, family, children, elderly, etc.). Thus, aspects of social policy can be found in several ministries. Social policy is often analysed using a large variety of disciplines in the analysis – such as combining a variety of the following theoretical approaches: economics, sociology, political science, anthropology, philosophy, history and law. One could, perhaps, argue that social policy analysis is, by now, a discipline in itself, as there often is a need to look into several disciplines in order to understand the development and the way the policy is decided, implemented and financed in different countries. Still, in most countries, the ministry of finance also influences policy by setting the budget for social policy.

There has been, and perhaps still is, confusion about what social policy is, and the concepts used might often be seen as vague (Béland and Petersen, 2014). Some examples of definitions are from a lecture of Richard Titmuss, who was professor of Social Administration at the London School of Economics:[1]

> Social Policies are concerned with the right ordering of the network of relationships between men and women who live together in societies, or with the principles which should govern the activities of individuals and groups so far as they affect the lives and interest of other people.
>
> (Macbeath, 1957, p. 212)

> Stated in general terms, the mainspring of social policy may be said to be the desire to ensure every member of the community certain minimum standards and certain opportunities.
>
> (Hagenbuch, 1958, p. 213)

> "Social Policy" is not a technical term with an exact meaning . . . it is taken to refer to the policy of governments with regard to action having a direct impact on the welfare of the citizen, by providing them with services or income. The central core consists, therefore of social

insurance, public (or national) assistance, the health and welfare services, housing policy.

(Marshall, 1965, p. 213)

Titmuss ended the lecture by arguing that "social policy is seen
to be beneficent, redistributive and concerned with economic as
well as non-economic objectives" (Alcock et al., 2001, p. 213).

Titmuss later argued that a question is also who does social
policy belong to and who is social policy aimed at? This is in the
context of policy being understood as the action to enable the
aims of the policy. Still, this also can imply that what for some
might be welfare, might for others be "illfare", for example, policy will have an impact on them they would have preferred to
avoid (Titmuss, 1974).

What constitutes the core of social policy can be difficult to
depict, but it can often be witnessed indirectly by the choice of a
more specific policy area. Often, it includes housing, education,
social security, social services and health (Drakeford, 2000). How
detailed and how many benefits and services to include can be
difficult to delimit, and, in fact, education is often outside the
scope of social policy analysis, despite the fact that the level of
education is often important in order to explain the individual's
position in society; and also in labour market policies, this is even
more important now than in the past.

Another very broad approach is when arguing that "broadly
speaking the study of social policy is the study of the role of
the state in relation to the welfare of its citizens" (Hill, 1996,
p. 3). However, this can, for example, also cause the use of public
spending in order to support voluntary organisations and the
family when supporting an individual. So, even if the main focus
is on the state, it implicitly also reaches out to the other agents
in society and their support to friends, families, etc.

Studying social policy also embraces many and varied approaches,
or to put it another way: "What makes social policy unusual is not
just that it makes no claims to distinctiveness, but that it is ready to
borrow from anywhere and everywhere it can in order to examine
its subject" and further that "Social policy is concerned with practical problems" (Spicker, 1995, p. 16).

In another book on social policy by Spicker, it is simply argued that "Social Policy entails the study of the social relations necessary for humans [*sic*] wellbeing and the systems by which wellbeing may be promoted" (Spicker, 2014, p. 1).

Thus, definitions and approaches are very wide; however, central notions revolve around how to ensure a decent living standard for many, including the impact on inequality and poverty, but also on well-being and everyday life in their broadest sense. Furthermore, it is focused on institutions, who is responsible and how is it financed. Based upon this broad and, admittedly, partly vague notion, this book tries to analytically describe and analyse what social policy in the confines of modern welfare states is.

Labour market policy is, in contrast to social policy, easier to define, as it revolves around how the labour market functions and what needs to be done in order to reduce unemployment, but also to ensure a continual high level of employment and debates on the generosity of benefits for those unemployed. The intersection on the level of benefits can be interpreted both as social and labour market policy, thus also being an argument for analysing these two concepts together.

## 1.4. OVERVIEW OF THE BOOK

This section gives an overview of what to expect in the following chapters of the book. The book is split so that Chapters 2 to 5 depict, analyse and present social policy; and the focus in Chapters 6 and 7 is on labour market policy, with Chapter 8 providing conclusions about social and labour market policy in modern societies, where industrial production is no longer the central approach to jobs and income.

Chapter 2 describes more clearly the various elements of social policy, while at the same time highlighting the variety of issues and core issues that can be found in the field of social policy, such as child, family, social security, housing, disability, health and long-term care (without going into detail), but providing the necessary background to understand why social policy is an important issue in these fields. It further provides definitions related to the distinction between benefits in kind, in cash and the variety of ways of providing and financing social policy. It also points to the variety of actors in the field and how they are, or might be, involved in delivering welfare. The distinction between public, fiscal and occupational welfare is included as a way of depicting a variety of ways of delivering social policy, thereby also emphasising the variety of approaches, because this might be framed by the willingness and ability to pay taxes and duties.

In Chapter 3, the focus moves to the possible aims of social policy. If a central aim is the enhancement of well-being (or welfare), the question is then what is important to look into in order to understand well-being, and ways to measure well-being. This is, however, not sufficient knowledge if one wants to change; in that case, one must also understand how different instruments might help in the development of well-being. This includes differences between diverse welfare state types and including examples hereof. The difference between old and new social risk is presented, as they often use different instruments to achieve policy aim, but also explain why there is a constant pressure for change in the structure and approach to social policy. Alleviating poverty and inequality can also be seen as a possible aim of social policy, and therefore the kind of approaches that can be used to reduce this are discussed. It is, however, contested how much and how strong state intervention should be in order to reduce the number of people at risk of living in poverty.

Welfare states have been argued to be in crisis for many years (OECD, 1981 as an example). A lack of legitimacy has been one issue. Another is the lack of financial means to develop and enhance social policy to cover the variety of needs. How to choose what type of social policy to implement with the best results has therefore become increasingly more important. Chapter 4 therefore probes into how to evaluate social policy, how to understand evaluation in the field, and also discusses the use and misuse of social policy evaluation as a way of developing the field. This also as recent years have seen a surge and focus on how to most effectively achieve the aims of social policy, given the pressure on welfare states' ability to finance social policy. Thus, there has been increased focus on what does and does not work, for example the movement towards evidence-based social policy. This is also a consequence of the fact that different approaches can have various impacts on users.

Social policy is not just decided and implemented. The field is laden with normative and ideological issues. Chapter 5 goes into why ideas and ideology are important issues to understand in relation to how systems develop and who the winners and losers are in this development. The chapter further touches upon old as well as new approaches in order to understand social policy. This includes a presentation and discussion of the Keynesian, neo-liberal and social-investment approaches. Last, the impact of regionalisation (EU) and globalisation are considered. Thus, ideas matter – and some of them influence social as well as labour market policy. This is therefore also a good link when moving, in Chapter 6, to a focus on labour market policy.

Whereas the subject of social policy is less strongly defined, labour market policy clearly revolves around how to under-stand the functioning of the labour market. Chapter 6 starts by describing what a labour market is – and also that it is not just one market, but many and varied types of markets. Under-standing changes on the labour market ranges from issues of explaining the level of employment in relation to the level of unemployment, and the possible reasons for this, to combin-ing it with how modern technology might influence the future development of the labour market, including concepts such as dualisation, insider/outsider and the precariat. Flexicurity is dis-cussed as a concept used in many countries, but also with strong degree of diversity as to what is actually included in and when discussing labour market policy. Links to discussions on social security benefits (unemployment and social assistance) are also given. Social dumping and the impact on migration are touched upon. In many countries, the central actors in labour market policy are the state, trade unions and employers' organisations. Therefore, the varied ways in which social partners are involved in developing working conditions, agreeing on wages and other issues for the development of the labour market are shown.

Having considered the understanding of what a labour market is and the central actors, Chapter 7 then moves the focus to what is labelled active labour market policy (ALMP). Since the 1950s in Sweden, there has been a long-tradition of ALMP – and also in the other Nordic countries in Europe. The chapter focuses on the rationales and logics behind ALMP, but the trend from broad-based types of activation to a work-first approach is also central to the chapter. The issue of life-long learning is also included. Additionally, it highlights and presents the knowledge of what does and does not work in ALMP. So even if some countries are actually pursuing an ALMP, this might not work due to, for example, the economic business cycle, if the aim is integration into the labour market. If the specific ALMP does not enable people to actually get a job, this might be activation for activation's sake. The different types of ALMP, their policy goals and possible impacts are shown.

Last, Chapter 8 wraps up the book and also includes a discussion on the possible future for social and labour market policy in a still more globalised and technologically advanced society. This includes how social and labour market policy is connected, together with a few more explorative remarks on future developments.

## 1.5. SOME DELIMITATIONS

Naturally, there are some delimitations in a book such as this.

Despite the fact that education plays a central role in acquiring the skills necessary to be able to make choices and have the necessary capabilities to be part of, and included in, society's development, this is not in any detail encompassed in this book. This, by itself, is a large and central policy area. However, in passing, reflection on life-long learning and upskilling as part of labour market policy is included.

The book, further, but to a more limited extent, presents a description of the specific systems in different countries. These descriptions of systems are at a general and more superficial level, in stages, by presenting data, for example, on the level of spending and in which areas, and thereby indicating variations and commonalities among countries. A few examples of institutional information and change in policy are also highlighted. For a recent overview of European welfare systems, see Schubert, Villota and Kuhlmann (2016).

The book also, to a more limited extent, points to and discusses whether and how international organisations might influence social and labour market policy by setting the discourse for policy, or, in relation to the EU, on the impact on nation states' ability to do what they would like to do in the field. However, as stated previously, a few words especially on the role of the EU are part of the presentation.

Welfare states and welfare state regimes have been core elements in many analyses over the last 25 years at least. Despite this, albeit presenting a few data from different countries, the focus of this book is not on the possible impact on, or the distinction among the countries belonging to, different welfare state regimes; instead, the aim in more general terms is to present how social and labour market policy has come into existence and what it is.

Methodologies and how to research in the field of social and labour market policy are outside the scope of this book; see, instead, Bryman (2015). Naturally, one cannot answer any question on social and labour market policy by using research without having a discussion on choice of theories and what methodology to use in order to be able to answer the question; however, for the purpose of this book, this is not important.

## 1.6. SUMMING UP

This chapter has set the scene for the book by presenting an overview of the book, while at the same time highlighting the actual definition of social and labour market policy. In a general way, these policies are enacted and developed in order to cope with our different needs for support over our lifetime – ranging from helping us into the world and having a good start in life, to care when we are old and frail. However, over the life course (Yerkes and Peper, 2018) nearly all will in some situation be in need of support – naturally some more than others as our individual abilities, as well as our preferences, are different. Social and labour market policy helps over the life course, but some who are more in need will often be supported more than others.

Policies vary across countries for historical and ideological reasons, as well as due to the differences in the economic options that are available. The book will limit the presentation of these differences; however, comparing one's own countries with others might help in understanding why there are differences, but also presumably in finding good solutions to the challenges there are over time in most countries.

## NOTE

1 The following are quotations from Alcock, P. et al., 2001.

## REFERENCES

Alcock, P. et al. (2001), *Welfare and Wellbeing: Richard Titmuss's Contribution to Social Policy*. Bristol, Policy Press.

Béland, D. and Petersen, K. (2014), *Analysing Social Policy Concepts and Language*. Bristol, Policy Press.

Bryman, A. (2015), *Social Research Methods*, 5th edition. Oxford, Oxford University Press.

Drakeford, M. (2000), *Privatisation and Social Policy*. Essex, Pearson Education Limited.

Esping-Andersen, G. ed. (1996), *Welfare States in Transition: National Adaptations in Global Economies*. London, Sage.

Esping-Andersen, G. (1999), *Social Foundations of Post-Industrial Economics*. Oxford, Oxford University Press.

Giddens, A. (1998), *The Third Way: The Renewal of Social Democracy*. Cambridge, Polity Press.

Hill, M. (1996), *Social Policy. A Comparative Analysis*. Hemel Hempstead, Harvester Wheatsheaf.

Miller, S. (1990), Evolving Welfare State Mixes in Evers, A. and Wintersberger, H. eds., *Shifts in the Welfare Mix: Their Impact on Work, Social Services and Welfare Policies*. Frankfurt, Boulder.

Morel, N., Palier B. and Palme J.(2012), *Towards a Social Investment Welfare State? Ideas, Policies and Challenges*. Bristol, Policy Press.

OECD. (1981), *The Welfare State in Crisis*. Paris, OECD.

Schubert, K., Villota, P. and Kuhlmann, J. (2016), *Challenges to European Welfare Systems*. Heidelberg, Springer.

Spicker, P. (1995), *Social Policy. Themes and Approaches*. Hemel Hempstead, Harvester Wheatsheaf.

Spicker, P. (2014), *Social Policy: Theory and Practice*, 3rd edition. Bristol, Policy Press.

Taylor-Gooby, P. ed. (2004), *New Risks, New Welfare: The Transformation of the European Welfare State*. Oxford, Oxford University Press.

Timmins, N. (1995), *The Five Giants: A Biography of the Welfare State*. London, Fontana Press.

Titmuss, R. M. (1974), *Social Policy*. London, George Allen & Unwin.

Yerkes, M. and Peper, B. (2018), Welfare States and the Life Course in Greve, B. ed., *Handbook of the Welfare State*, 2nd edition. Oxon, Routledge.

## 2

# ELEMENTS OF SOCIAL POLICY

## 2.1. INTRODUCTION

This chapter highlights the variety of issues and possible elements that can be found in the field of social policy, such as child, family, social security, housing, disability, health and long-term care (without going into detail, but providing the necessary background to understand why social policy is an important issue). It further provides definitions related to the distinction between benefits in kind, in cash and the variability of ways of providing and financing social policy.

It also points to the variety of actors in the field and how they are, or might be, involved in delivering welfare, thus also highlighting a central discussion in social policy – the boundaries between state and civil society, and the role of the market, which has been increasing in many countries.

Since way back to Richard M. Titmuss's presentation of the many and varied ways to finance and deliver welfare, there has been a distinction between public, fiscal and occupational welfare. This area is included as a way of depicting the variety and complexity in the many ways of delivering and financing social policy.

Many of the issues and concepts presented in this chapter are "timeless", in the sense that they have been in existence for many years, and are seemingly important even when societies change, and also if new types of employment or living conditions are under development.

## 2.2. CENTRAL FIELDS IN SOCIAL POLICY

How to distinguish between different aims and approaches, and how to look into variations and what is, in fact, included in social policy is not always clear. One way to do this is to look into a variety of sectors:

a) Social insurance
b) Social assistance
c) Publicly funded social services
d) Social work and personal social services
e) Economic governance

(Garland, 2016, p. 46)

In a way this reflects historical approaches, as social insurance was one of the first issues, and the personal social service and economic governance were among the latecomers. There can be, and are, varied sub-sectors in the five sectors (see previous), and also a division of who pays. The fact that there has been change in the understanding of the state's role over time is exemplified in the following quotes:[1]

> The Government accept as one of their primary aims and responsibilities of a high and stable level of employment.
>
> (UK Employment Policy White Paper, 1944)

> What is the economic function of the state, of any modern state? It is first, a relative redistribution of income; second a subsidy in the form of production of collective goods; and third, a regulation of economic processes ensuring full growth and full employment.
>
> (French Finance Minister, Giscard D'Estaing, 1972)

> Welfare benefits, distributed with little or no consideration of their effects on behavior, encourage legitimacy, facilitated the breakdown of families, and replaced incentives favouring work and self-reliance with perverse encouragement for idleness and cheating.
>
> (Margaret Thatcher, 1993)

The previous quotes indicate that social and labour market policy in welfare states can be understood to range from having a positive role, to a situation where welfare benefits might have a negative impact on individuals' behaviour, including that some are cheating the system.

Here, the focus is on the ways to welfare, who provides the welfare, and the principles on which this is based. The principles can also be understood as having a focus on welfare for the poor (Garland, 2014). The ways to welfare can have different impacts, including an impact on who is able to receive the benefits, the distributional outcome of the different benefits and the financial impact on the public sector. This is an important aspect of social policy.

Titmuss was the first to point to the three different ways to welfare: public, fiscal and occupational welfare (Titmuss, 1958; see also Sinfield, 2018, Farnsworth, 2018 and Alcock et al., 2001). The three ways can, but need not, be supplementary, or interacting with each other. They can also be a substitute for each other.

Public welfare is the welfare paid for, but not necessarily delivered, by the public sector. Access to benefits is often dependent on being a citizen or having a legal right to stay in a country. There can be, and in fact are, many criteria for receiving benefits (see also Section 2.3), with sometimes historical reasons for a country using and defining criteria in a specific way. It is often registered as public spending, and we have an abundant number of data available in national countries' statistics, in the EU and the OECD to mention just a few possible sources, and also in online data. It is welfare paid for mainly by taxes and duties; however, there is a variation in user charges from zero to full payment, so the mix in payment of welfare will vary across countries. In many of the central fields described later, it is mainly public welfare we have solid information and data about; see, on financing, Morel and Palme (2018).

In contrast to public welfare, occupational welfare relates to what a person on the labour market gets paid for by the employer when having a job. This can be different kinds of social insurance. Although it is labelled social insurance, despite this name it is not individual, and payment does not depend on the individual's risk profile, but the criteria for receiving benefits will be the same for all. Thus, in many ways, when it is obligatory social insurance, it resembles public welfare, although those who can receive the benefit might vary. Payments into pension savings and health are among the central aspects paid for by occupational welfare. As employers can deduct the expenses, part of the payment is indirectly paid for by all taxpayers as it reduces the revenue that would otherwise be received by the public sector. In this way, there is an indirect connection between the state and occupational welfare, which blurs who, in fact, is paying for the welfare, and there is also variation across social policy areas. Occupational welfare tends to have an upside-down effect; for example those with higher wages and stable jobs have more occupational welfare than those with low-income and unstable jobs. For a recent overview, see the special issue of *Social Policy & Administration*, Vol. 52, No. 2, 2018 and Farnsworth (2018).

Fiscal welfare relates to the deductions that can be made in the tax system, for example, when paying into a pension fund, in-work tax-credits or health/sickness insurance. Fiscal welfare is defined as deviations from the normal tax system when not all taxpayers can use it, and this is often labelled the hidden welfare state (Howard, 1997). Fiscal welfare can also be labelled as tax expenditures. As stated previously, fiscal welfare tends to have an upside-down effect, implying that those with the highest income gain the most from the use of fiscal welfare. Naturally, this depends on the national system and traditions, so in principle only a specific empirical analysis can depict the degree of inequality arising from the use of fiscal welfare. The reason it is characterised as hidden is that there is no direct way in statistics to find the size of the hidden welfare state, and in most countries no official statistics are available. It is further hidden in the sense that public welfare will have to be decided every year, whereas fiscal welfare continues until a law with the inbuilt tax rebate is changed or the tax rate used for the calculation is changed; see also Sinfield (2018).

These three ways can be combined in several ways. This, again, is an issue for empirical analysis.

Historically, welfare states developed with a focus on income transfers, such as in relation to unemployment, old age, industrial injury and sickness. The variation and ways in which welfare states were financed and structured varied from country to country. Thus, different kinds of services were not – except for education, if this is understood as social policy – part of public welfare. The size of the benefit was not large, and only a limited number of social contingencies were covered. The limited number of benefits and the size hereof reflects the fact that social policy is often connected to how rich countries are. So after the Second World War when societies became richer, welfare states were expanded in many and different areas.

Those in need of services were taken care of in the family (children and the elderly), and, at the same time, life expectancy was much lower than it is today so the need for long-term care was less in demand than today. People with disabilities were often left to be taken care of in the family.

Men were seen as those providing income – therefore, the welfare system was considered as a male-breadwinner system. Women took care of the household and the family, and children started working at a younger age than today. Gradually, when women also entered the labour market, and to a different degree in various countries, there was a need to develop a system that could help take care of children and elderly dependants. Therefore, over time, different kinds of services entered the social policy area. The Nordic welfare states in Europe were among the first to have substantial child-care arrangements, and, therefore, they were argued to be the first to develop service welfare states. Care has gradually been expanding in many countries, but often with a high level of user charges.

One service area that was developed early was the health care system, and hospitals and general practitioners were – again, to a different degree in dissimilar countries – developed; see also Wendt (2018).

As countries became gradually more affluent, there came a wish to support the development of children's lives, and family allowances in different forms were introduced into the systems. They were often higher for younger children than for older children, and in some countries they were higher when having more children, and the reverse in other countries. So, again, we have very diverse systems and traditions in order to help families with children.

Maternity and paternity leave were also introduced gradually into the welfare systems, showing that social policy is a patchwork of diverse types of benefits and services that can vary between countries. It is further an area where, in many countries, systems developed even in times described as times of austerity, and also with different emphases and criteria for receiving benefits and/or services.

Table 2.1 shows for the EU28 the percentages of GDP of the different social policy functions (including unemployment) using the EU's ESSPROS (European system of integrated social protection statistics) system; the different types are explained in more detail in Section 2.3.

Table 2.1 shows that, despite the financial crisis in 2008/2009, social protection has on average as a percentage of GDP increased in the EU28. Part of this reflects the fact that GDP fell in 2009 and 2010, and thus the same amount of money spent on social protection looks like an increase in spending as a percentage of GDP. However, there has also been in real prices an increase in spending per head on average in the 28 countries. Sometimes, there can also be, and are, large differences in development among countries due to differing ideological, economic and political reasons (see also Chapter 5), and therefore some countries with retrenchment.

*Table 2.1*  Social protection spending in the EU28 as % of GDP using ESSPROS main groups

| EU28 | 2008 | 2010 | 2012 | 2014 |
|---|---|---|---|---|
| Total | 24.8 | 27.4 | 27.6 | 27.6 |
| Sickness/health care | 7.3 | 8.0 | 8.0 | 8.1 |
| Disability | 1.9 | 2.1 | 2.0 | 2.0 |
| Old age | 9.8 | 10.7 | 11.0 | 11.1 |
| Survivors | 1.5 | 1.6 | 1.6 | 1.6 |
| Family/children | 2.1 | 2.4 | 2.3 | 2.4 |
| Unemployment | 1.3 | 1.7 | 1.5 | 1.4 |
| Housing | 0.5 | 0.6 | 0.6 | 0.6 |
| Social exclusion | 0.5 | 0.5 | 0.5 | 0.5 |

Source: Eurostat, spr_exp_gdp, accessed the 2nd of May, 2017

The following shows the development in spending per head since the financial crisis (in both yearly prices and fixed 2010 prices in euros):

*Table 2.2*    Development in spending per head since the financial crisis

| Social protection expenditure per head | 2008 | 2010 | 2012 | 2014 |
|---|---|---|---|---|
| EU (28 countries) 2010 prices | 6,482.97 | 6,978.88 | 6,999.50 | 7,116.75 |
| EU (28 countries) yearly prices | 6,471.63 | 6,978.88 | 7,349.55 | 7,609.87 |

Source: Eurostat, spr_exp_gdp, accessed the 2nd of May, 2017

Thus, when looking at the fixed 2010 prices, the development has been rather modest, and the main increase was seemingly decided before the breakout of the last financial crisis or because of the growing unemployment in 2009/2010; whereas in each year's prices, there has been an increase. Measuring per head only gives an indication of the overall development, not necessarily how it is perceived by the users and recipients as there might have been an increase in people in need of support (e.g. due to more elderly and/or an increase in the level of unemployment). The data might further blur the development between different sub-sections of social and labour market policy; for example an increase is possible in one area, while at the same time there is retrenchment in other areas.

Table 2.1 further shows that the central social policy area when looking at public welfare is sickness/health care and old age. It is in these fields that the welfare states spend the main part of the expenditures. Especially in the field of old age, there have been increases in the level of spending, presumably as a consequence of the demographic ageing of the population in Europe, and this change in demography might also have influenced spending on health care – again, despite people in general being healthier in old age than previously.

When comparing across countries, there is one further caveat with regard to the level as a percentage of GDP and when measuring the generosity of the benefits. This is whether or not the benefits are counted as taxable income, and, thereby, that the welfare state gets part of the benefit back in income tax. This is often the case with unemployment benefit (but varies considerably among countries), whereas family allowances are often not taxable income. Therefore, countries that might look like high-level spenders are not necessarily so; see also Adema, Fron and Ladaique (2011).

Recent years have also seen a growing focus on how to integrate refugees and migrants in different countries, thereby adding a new field to the social policy area. Integration into both the social and labour markets is a further contested issue, including how this integration influences other citizens.

## 2.3. BASIC CONCEPTS

The following presents several basic concepts that are used when unfolding and trying to understand social policy issues. Although the conditions for receiving the various benefits and the way in which they are received can be many and very different, the concepts are in themselves not influenced by the development of the actual implementation of social policies, as they merely point to possible varieties and ways of carrying out social policy.

Benefits can be either universal or selective. If a benefit is seen as universal, it depends, first, on citizenship and/or the legal right to stay in a country, although a broader understanding was the one Titmuss presented, "the aim of making services available and accessible to the whole population in such ways as would not involve users in any humiliating loss of status, dignity or self-respect" (Titmuss, 1968, p. 129). This broader interpretation also has a focus on the consequences of receiving benefits; for example, there should not be any negative aspect related to receiving the benefit, including shame. Without arguing it, behind the quotation is also an aspect that those receiving universal benefit were deserving; see also Chapters 4 and 5. Framing recipients as scroungers and/or lazy, including the use of the description "welfare tourist", are indicators that not everyone supports a universal approach to welfare benefits, and some find that benefits as a whole are not paid out only to needy people.

Universalism thus also revolves around whether everyone is covered based upon citizenship or residency, but it can be modified in the way benefits are allocated in different ways (Frederiksen, 2017).

This can be seen by the fact that even if a benefit is universal, criteria can be attached which should be fulfilled in order to receive the possible benefit. In most welfare states, access to hospitals when in acute need of treatment is a universal service. Receiving unemployment benefit (see also Chapter 6) is often combined with the demand that persons receiving the benefit shall actively search for a job, and be willing, in many countries, to take any available job.

A selective benefit depends on being a member of, or having paid into, a social insurance fund (or similar). Access to benefit in the Bismarckian social insurance system is as described in Chapter 1. There might be derived rights from membership of a social insurance fund, such as even if only one member of the family is insured, there can also be right of coverage for other members of the family. This is, for example, the case in most central European obligatory social insurance systems, where historically women were also covered in case of sickness and old age even if only the man had a job (as was the case most of the time).

A central distinction is between benefits in cash and in kind. Benefits in cash is money paid out to those eligible for the benefit. There are typically conditions related to receiving these benefits, and they might even be restricted to be used within or for a certain purpose, sometimes in the way of a voucher; however, most of the time, cash benefits can be used by the recipients in any way they would like; see also Matsaganis (2018).

Two contradictory arguments are at play here. One being that cash makes it possible for the individual to be able to make his/her own choice of combination of goods and services. Thus, the state (or insurance company) does not enter into what the individual can use the money for.

In contrast, it is argued that giving cash (instead of services or with a strong restriction on how the benefits can be used) risks that the individual will make choices not in accordance with what those financing the benefit would prefer the money to be used for. This, for example, could be the case if a drug-addict uses social assistance to buy drugs. This is a more paternalistic approach, and can have an impact on the legitimacy of the chosen policy; see also Chapter 4.

Benefits in kind is a group of different services financed mainly by the state; however, they can be delivered by the state, non-governmental organisations (NGOs) or private for or non-profit companies. The benefits can be in the form of child care, long-term care or health care where a person is given access if in need of the service. They can also be in the form of a right to receive welfare service from different providers, thereby giving the freedom to choose among providers of the good; again, this can be public as well as private. As argued, choice can be seen to be positive for the individual, such as benefits in cash, by making it possible to get service closer to one's preferences, albeit individuals are not always able to make informed choices (Greve, 2010).

The size and criteria for access to benefits in kind and in cash can vary. Table 2.3 shows a variety of possible criteria in order to receive central in-kind and in-cash benefits.

Child benefits or family allowances together with old age pensions are the best examples of age-related benefits. In both cases, they can be given with or without being means-tested. A means-tested benefit is dependent on income and/or wealth or other criteria informing on the individual's situation. The opposite is a non-means-tested benefit, which is a benefit not dependent on the person's income and/or wealth. For family allowances, an argument that they should be non-means tested is that this is a support for the extra cost for families with children

*Table 2.3*    Possible criteria for access to in-kind and in-cash benefits in welfare states

|  | Examples in-kind | Examples in-cash |
| --- | --- | --- |
| Age | Day care for children | Pension, child benefits |
| Unemployed | Training/education in some countries | Unemployment benefit |
| Need | Long-term care | Social assistance |
| Sick | Hospitals | Sickness benefit |
| Low income | Cheaper/free medicine, | Social assistance, |
| Non-work ability/people with disabilities | Different kind of help-remedies | Early retirement/ disability pension |

Source: Own depiction

not dependent on their overall economic situation, and a transfer from families without children to families with children. The same is often used as an argument for support to people with disabilities – that the support should enable them to be on an equal position with people without disabilities, and thus even if they earn income or have a fortune, they have the right to the benefit.

Whether the means-test is based upon the individual and/or family situation depends on the national system. Housing allowances are often based upon the family's situation, whereas other benefits can be related to the position of the individual, such as unemployment benefit.

There will always be arguments in favour of and against the way means-tested benefits are used. They range from administrative (it is simpler without a test and based on the use of a few simple criteria only), to equality (why give to already rich people), to the level of expenditure (using means-testing can reduce overall cost).

One can further argue that access to benefits is dependent on different understandings of what justice is. A needs approach would use and focus on means-testing, whereas a merit approach would use social insurance so that when a specific contingency occurs, access to benefit is possible, whereas equality often uses universal access, including trying to reduce inequality in society.

Another distinction is between discretionary and non-discretionary benefits.

Discretionary benefits are when the social administrator can decide whether a person has a right to receive a benefit, and perhaps even the level and type of support available. It can also be negatively defined as discretionary, which means that sanctions can be imposed (by reducing the benefit) especially for those receiving social assistance or unemployment benefit if they are not active enough in their search for a job or in their participation in different kinds of activation.

Non-discretionary benefits are benefits where, if specified contingencies occur, the individual has access to benefits at a pre-defined level – at an absolute level, percentage of previous income, size of the family, etc. In these cases, the social administrator determines only whether or not the situation that gives access to a benefit has been fulfilled.

The tendency has been towards non-discretionary benefits, as this is much simpler to administer, and avoids the risk that social workers favour certain groups compared to others, albeit with the possible negative consequence that the ability to look into a more holistic approach to social policy needs can be difficult. However, if there are many criteria attached to receiving benefits, this can also be difficult to administer and difficult for people to understand.

The welfare states service areas, using the ESSPROS division of areas, includes subjects such as long-term care/old age care, child care/family policy. ESSPROS is a good way to get structured information on the rules, institutional approach and central conditions attached to the variety of services (as well as benefits) in all the EU-member states, and is updated every six months. Thus, looking into this information also clearly shows the large variety in organisation, financing and conditions for various social policy issues. For other countries, OECD or national websites are good points of reference.

Sickness/health care is, as shown in Table 2.1, the second largest social policy field when measured as spending as a proportion of GDP. Health care is another example of a service area that, in most countries, is characterised as universal, so that citizens and legal residents in need of hospital treatment have access, and the right, to treatment. This can be, and is often, combined with different kinds of user charges, for example when visiting a general practitioner or buying medicine. In addition, access to private hospitals and different specialists might only be possible if the individual is insured or can afford to pay. So, despite universality in access to hospitals, there might overall be inequality in access to health care, also evidenced in many countries by the inequality in life expectancy among different groups.

In most countries, people with disabilities also get access to benefits and services without any specific means-test, which are dependent on the severity of their disability. The level and kind of support varies across countries. The reason why it is not means-tested is, presumably, due to two different, but interrelated, reasons – one being that people with disabilities are seen as deserving, and that their need is not due to their own fault. Furthermore, for reasons of justice, the support is often free of charge. This because it is a way of attempting to make the living conditions and options for one's preferred life the same for people with and without different degrees of disabilities. This is not to say that people with disabilities have the same options, as they, for example, less often get an education or a job on the labour market.

Pensions to the elderly (and people on early retirement pensions) is one of the largest spending areas in most welfare states. This is due to the demographic structure of societies with an increasing number of elderly. For the same reason, there have been a number of pension reforms in several countries with the aim of increasing the pensionable age, changing the conditions for receiving benefits, and, in many countries, changing the system from a pay-as-you-go (PAYG) system to one that is at least partly funded. The calculation of benefit has also, in many countries, changed from being a percentage of final salary or a fixed amount when retiring, to being, in many ways, dependent on how much has been put into a person's pension funds during the working life.

Thus, the pension system has undergone strong changes in recent years, with the aim of reducing the pressure on the public sector economy both now and even more so in the years to come. A more indirect issue has been to try to get people to stay on the labour market longer, as people now live longer and are healthier than they used to be. The generosity of the level of pension also varies strongly across countries (see also Hinrichs, 2018).

Sickness was also one of the first social risks to be covered, and today in most countries there is some coverage in case of sickness. Systems vary to a large extent – from pure state systems, combined state and market (often through collective agreements), to market-based systems, where the individual takes out his/her own insurance. The size of the coverage, and thereby the replacement rate (see later), also varies across systems. Thus, only a detailed analysis of different countries' systems is able to inform on the generosity or lack thereof in the different welfare states' coverage of loss of income due to sickness.

Maternity and paternity leave, although becoming a parent is not a sickness, is often related to sickness benefits and with the same type of coverage.

The sickness and leave benefit systems also inform us that the sheer number of people on social policy benefits, in itself, does not necessarily provide information about the problems of integration into society or on the labour market. This is because being on a benefit or on leave for a short while does not provide information on the long-term position. Thus, looking at the number of persons on different social benefits needs to be split into different categories in order to be able to have an idea about the possible need for societal intervention in order to increase social integration.

This is also part of the debate on the degree of social exclusion and/or social inclusion. These two types of concepts are, in reality, closely related; albeit, for some, it seems better to talk positively on how to include people, whereas the inclusion of some people often causes the exclusion of others. Still, social policy is also about social cohesion and social integration. This can be supported by several of the various benefits as mentioned previously; however, the risk can also be reduced by prevention.

Conceptually, prevention refers to the fact that in certain circumstances it might be possible to prevent a certain social condition from occurring, and thereby reducing damage and the need for intervention (Debels and Van Hoyweghen, 2018). This can range from preventing diseases and accidents at workplaces, to investment in children's development, thereby preventing young people from not getting an education. This might even be economically beneficial for the welfare state (Heckman, 2006).

However, even if systems are in place, it might not be all who get the benefit. The number of those eligible who get the benefit is called the take-up rate, and the higher the rate, the more people get the benefit they are entitled to. It can be difficult to depict its size or estimate it as some claimants might not ask for a benefit because there might be stigma attached to receiving benefits (Currie, 2004), albeit automatic enrolment and payment of benefits can reduce the possible stigma.

Besides stigma, very low replacement rates might also imply a risk of low take-up rate. The replacement rate is the level of benefit compared to income when being on the labour market. This will mainly be calculated by taking the level of the specific benefit and the impact of the tax system into consideration, but not necessarily other welfare benefits. For example, even if the unemployment benefit is low compared to previous income, the reduction in disposable income might be influenced by other types of benefits (housing benefits, family allowances or other specific benefits or services). Therefore, the comparison of replacement rates might sometimes need to be related to other parts of the social policy system rather than just one benefit in order to fully understand whether and how this influences the level of poverty and inequality; see also Chapter 3.

The level of the replacement rate is a good indicator of how generous and encompassing social policy is. However, in recent years, (see also Chapters 6 and 7, especially with regard to unemployment benefit and social assistance) there has been a debate on the incentives to take up a job if the replacement rate is seen as being too "high". There is, theoretically, no clear knowledge of what a too-high level of benefit is; this is due to that not only are people influenced by economic incentives, but also aspects such as social contacts, having something to do (Brooks, 2011).

Social security can be seen as an overarching concept, where "the right to social security encompasses the right to access and maintain benefits, whether in cash or in kind without discrimination in order to secure protection" (Pennings, 2018, paragraph 2). Protection can then be related to the various situations as mentioned previously, but also access to health care and family support.

Last, another central concept is the degree of decommodification, which refers to the ability to maintain a decent living in a welfare state without having to sell one's labour on the market.

## 2.4. CORE ACTORS IN SOCIAL POLICY

The specific core actors vary from country to country. However, there are some overarching trends and specific actors influencing policy. They are different at the supranational, national, regional and local levels, reliant on the administrative and political structure in each country. Thus, the stakeholders are many and varied. They can and have different preferences and interests, and they can be stronger or weaker in their ability to influence social policy development.

In Europe, the EU (see also, especially, Chapter 6), in principle, only has limited competences in the field of social policy, but by using the open method of coordination (OMC) (De La Porte, 2018), a focus on what works best and the European Social Fund, it tries to influence development in the member states. The limited formal competence is also the reason why this is presented here only to a more limited extent, and why the focus instead is on national types of actors. Many national actors, especially in larger countries, will have regional and local affiliations.

In most welfare states, the state is the central actor as it sets the national rules related to who can get what kind of benefit and under what conditions (see earlier in the chapter). It is also the state which sets the rules and levels of financing of the social policy. Thus, other actors often try to influence policymakers at the central level. This can be related to overall level of spending, size of benefit, eligibility criteria for receiving benefits, new types of services needed, etc. This also includes several think tanks, which can have different political or economic interests in pursuing a specific policy in the field.

Albeit the state has the central role in many countries, the regions and/or municipalities also have a role in the daily administration and delivery of services. The stronger the role for the local regions and municipalities, the more likely it is that there are local actors which can be an affiliation of central actors.

NGOs often have a role as pressure groups for developing an area, and often they deliver the service themselves.

Historically, the church often played a central role in providing food and shelter for those most in need. The church still has a role (varying from country to country) of different sizes and types, ranging from still providing services and benefits, to being an advocacy group.

Informal care plays a central role in several areas. This can be provided by family/friends, but also sometimes by voluntary people. Thus, as voters and in different kinds of organisations, they can influence social policy. Informal care must be seen not only as an actor, but also as a provider of social welfare.

In many countries, labour market partners often have, especially in relation to labour market development and policy, a very strong role, but also in the field of social policy there can be a role. Occupational welfare is thus often combined with fiscal welfare decided by the partners (or alone by the employer), thereby influencing the state social policy. Saving for pension purposes is a good example of provision in the field of social policy. Occupational based pensions also show how there can be a connection between the state and the market, by that the state ensures a basic minimum level of benefit, whereas when having a job there will be increased level of pension. This can imply higher levels of inequality (see further Chapter 3) but also increased difference between the core and periphery on the labour market (see Chapter 6).

Further, in relation to labour market development, collective agreements in several countries play a central role in setting the level of wages and working conditions. Stability on the labour market can also be part of what the partners help in ensuring. The trade unions' role has, in several countries, been weakened over the last 10–20 years. The relation between state, employers and employees can be labelled corporatism.

With the increased marketisation of service delivery in many countries, private providers might also have a voice, and try to influence the development of social policy in such a way that they can have a larger share of the market and make a profit from the way in which they deliver goods and services. There are both providers with the aim of making a profit and non-profit providers, and this varies across countries. The many and varied private actors also imply that steering and ensuring quality especially in the delivery of welfare service can be difficult.

That welfare can be delivered both by the state, the market and within the civil society is often labelled the welfare mix. There is no firm theoretical knowledge on how the mix between these different actors role shall be in order to optimise welfare for a society. This is further not only related to who shall do the delivery, but also the financing of social policy. The mix varies further between different countries – often more important in the Southern and Eastern part of Europe, whereas the market plays a strong role within the more liberal welfare countries, and in the Northern and Central Europe the welfare state has a stronger role. The division between state, market and civil society is further influenced by ideas (see further in Chapter 5) and has also historically changed in many countries. Just as one example, earlier, children were always taken care of within the family; however today many countries have developed day care for children, albeit with differences in terms of who is delivering it (market or state) and also with regard to how expensive it is to have a child taken care of when being on the labour market. User charges (in public as well as private delivery) thus also influence the access to services in part of what the welfare states deliver.

Social policy has also developed with new social risks (see further in Chapter 3), so that what earlier was seen as something social policy should not do, has come on the agenda.

## 2.5. SUMMING UP

Social policy is a wide-ranging field with many rules and criteria related to who can get benefits and services, for how long and under what conditions. This varies across countries, and includes differences in the degree of means-testing (if at all) and the generosity of the benefits (e.g. replacement rate of benefit) when certain social contingency occurs. The level and types of services in areas such as health care, long-term care and child care are also very diverse across countries. Health care is often universal, whereas child care often can be very different with both state and market being actors, and also often comes with very different kinds and levels of user charges.

There are many and varied concepts indicating the complexity of the field; however they are helpful in order to have a knowledge about what can be central issues within social policy.

The rules and rights to benefits are constantly changing in most countries. There are a variety of possible reasons for this, some related to the fiscal constraints on the welfare states, some due to changes in the perception of who deserves and who does not deserve welfare benefits, and others due to new conditions in society, for example, on the labour markets (see Chapters 6 and 7). Thus even when having clear and defined concepts, there is at the same time room for making national decisions, and in some countries further on the regional/local level. This implies that access to benefits and services can vary, which might imply different degrees of inequality.

The many and varied actors in the different countries, including the mix between state, market and civil society, all help to explain the diversity of systems and the way they are structured. There is no clear knowledge about how to best have this mix, and, it further is often under constant change. Marketisation has, for example, been on the agenda for some years by now, albeit also with discussion of the possible consequences hereof.

Despite recent years' focus on marketisation, it is so that historically, the way social policy has developed shows that the state over the long run has a still more central role, especially in relation to those most at risk of social exclusion and a life in poverty.

## NOTE

1 The following are quotations from Garland (2016, pp. 57 and 107).

## REFERENCES

Adema, W., Fron, P. and Ladaique, M. (2011), Is the European Welfare State Really More Expensive? Indicators on Social Spending, 1980–2012 and a Manual to the OECD Social Expenditure. Database (SOCX). OECD Social, Employment and Migration Working Paper, No. 124, Paris, OECD.

Alcock, P. et al. (2001), *Welfare and Wellbeing: Richard Titmuss's Contribution to Social Policy*. Bristol, Policy Press.

Brooks, D. (2011), *The Social Animal: The Hidden Sources of Love, Character and Achievement*. New York, Random House.

Currie, J. (2004), The Take-Up of Social Benefits, Discussion Paper No. 1103, April 2004, Bonn, IZA.

Debels, A., and Van Hoyweghen, I. (2018), Prevention in Greve, B. ed., *Routledge International Handbook of the Welfare State*, 2nd edition. Abingdon, Routledge.

De La Porte, C. (2018), Social OMCs: Ideas, Politics and Effects in Greve, B. ed., *Routledge International Handbook of the Welfare State*, 2nd edition. Abingdon, Routledge.

Farnsworth, K. (2018), Occupational Welfare in Greve, B. ed., *Routledge International Handbook of the Welfare State*, 2nd edition. Abingdon, Routledge.

Frederiksen, M. (2017), Varieties of Scandinavian Universalism: A Comparative Study of Welfare Justifications. *Acta Sociologica*, pp. 1–14. doi: 10.117/0001699317699258.

Garland, D. (2014), The Welfare State: A Fundamental Dimension of Modern Government. *European Journal of Sociology*, vol. 55, no. 3, pp. 327–364.

Garland, D. (2016), *The Welfare State: A Very Short Introduction*. Oxford, Oxford University Press.

Greve, B. ed. (2010), *Choice: Challenges and Perspectives for the European Welfare States*. West-Sussex, Wiley-Blackwell.

Heckman, J. (2006), Skill Formation and the Economics of Investing in Disadvantaged Children. *Science*, New Series, vol. 312, no. 5782, pp. 1900–1902.

Hinrichs, K. (2018), Old Age and Pensions, in Greve, B. ed., *Routledge International Handbook of the Welfare State*, 2nd edition. Abingdon, Routledge.

Howard, C. (1997), *The Hidden Welfare State: Tax-Expenditures and Social Policy in the United States*. Princeton, NJ, Princeton University Press.

Matsaganis, M. (2018), Benefits in Kind and In Cash in Greve, B. ed., *Routledge International Handbook of the Welfare State*, 2nd edition. Abingdon, Routledge.

Morel, N. and Palme, J. (2018), Financing the Welfare State and the Politics of Taxation in Greve, B. ed., *Routledge International Handbook of the Welfare State*, 2nd edition. Abingdon, Routledge.

Pennings, F. (2018), Social Security in Greve, B. ed., *Routledge International Handbook of the Welfare State*, 2nd edition. Abingdon, Routledge.

Sinfield, A. (2018), Fiscal Welfare in Greve, B. ed., *Routledge International Handbook of the Welfare State*, 2nd edition. Abingdon, Routledge.

Titmuss, R. (1968), *Commitment to Welfare*. London, Allen & Unwin.

Titmuss, R. M. (1958), *Essays on 'The Welfare State'*. London, Allen & Unwin.

Wendt, C. (2018), Health Care in Greve, B. ed., *Routledge International Handbook of the Welfare State*, 2nd edition. Abingdon, Routledge.

# AIMS OF SOCIAL POLICY

## 3.1. INTRODUCTION

In this third chapter, the focus is on the possible aim of social policy. Historically, the focus was on ensuring basic needs, such as food and shelter. Later on, alleviating poverty came into focus. Today, this is not the only focus; well-being and welfare in a broader sense are also central to social policy.

If a central aim is the enhancement of well-being (or welfare), the question is then what is important to look into in order to understand well-being. Further, whether it is possible and whether there are different ways to measure well-being, and what policy recommendation that can lead to. However, this is not sufficient knowledge if one wants to change policy; in that case, one will also have to understand how different instruments might help in the development of well-being; for example, what is the impact of spending on policies to increased well-being, who pays the taxes to finance the welfare, etc.? This chapter also includes, albeit briefly, a presentation of the differences between diverse welfare states types and examples of instruments used. The different means used to achieve the aims of the old and new social risks are presented as they sometimes use different instruments, but also explain why there is constant pressure for change in the structure and approach to social policy.

Alleviating poverty and inequality can also be seen, as indicated previously, a possible aim of social policy. Therefore, it is important to know how to measure the different approaches that can be used to change poverty and equality (see the discussion in Section 3.5). It is contested how strong state intervention shall be in order to reduce the number of people at risk of living in poverty, and what the level of inequality shall be. Nevertheless, it is central to understand the mechanism and approaches hereto.

## 3.2. WHAT ARE WELL-BEING AND WELFARE?

Historically, the aim of the welfare state focused on how to ensure food and shelter for the poor, with what was then named the poor laws. Receiving benefit was filled with stigma, and the benefit was at a very low level. Thus, Maslow's Hierarchy of Needs (Maslow, 1943), as indicated in Figure 3.1, where it is first necessary to meet basic needs, and then when they are fulfilled, other needs become more important. Later, this was followed by Erik Allardt's "having, loving and being" (Allardt, 1993) as another way of expressing that some basic issues need

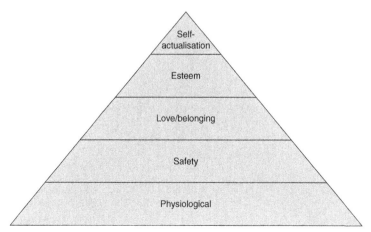

*Figure 3.1*   Maslow's Hierarchy of Needs
Source: Own depiction

to be fulfilled before it is possible to move to a higher level of well-being.

Figure 3.1 indicates that, first, there is a need to fulfil basic physiological needs; when this is done, other quality aspects of life are also possible; and, gradually, one might move upwards towards self-actualisation. Still, what this implies for the individual can, and will, be different as we as individuals have dissimilar preferences. Therefore, what might be very important for one person might not necessarily be so for someone else. Allardt also combined having, loving and being with objective and subjective indicators; see Table 3.1.

Table 3.1 further introduces the fact that the measure of quality of life/well-being is not only dependent on, and can be measured by, objective indicators, but also because people also relate to each other, so that individuals' relative position is important. Furthermore, as people have differences in their preferences and values related to their daily life, the same aspects will not be important for all. Thus, in relation to quality of life, objective measures (such as GDP, poverty rate, housing conditions, etc.) are not the only important aspects of developing well-being in a country; it is also important for people to have someone to talk to, and like the neighbourhood one is living in, etc. There is by now an abundant number of indexes, depictions and measurements of well-being (Greve, 2017).

Well-being theory would include five aspects as being important: "positive emotion, engagement or flow, positive relationships, meaning or purpose, and achievement" (Adler and

*Table 3.1*  Objective and subjective indicators related to having, loving and being

|  | *Objective indicators* | *Subjective indicators* |
|---|---|---|
| Having (material and impersonal needs) | The level of living and environmental conditions | Subjective feelings of dissatisfaction/satisfaction with living conditions |
| Loving (social needs) | Relationships to other people | Unhappiness/happiness – feelings on social relations |
| Being (needs for personal growth) | People's relation to society and nature | Feelings of alienation/personal growth |

Source: Allardt (1993, p. 93; slightly modified)

Seligman, 2016, p. 5). In line with Allardt and positive psychology, Adler and Seligman also suggest elements such as "meaning of life, purpose, autonomy, competence, self-realization, mindfulness, self-acceptance, authenticity, value congruence, and social connectedness" (p. 5).

Where it might be possible for welfare states to measure and do something, including the development of policies in relation to objective indicators, this might be more difficult to do related to the subjective issues as described in the preceding paragraph. Albeit, the line is not so straightforward, as illustrated in the following example. In many countries, loneliness is a problem – for the young as well as the elderly – and as social connection is important, this might be a policy issue. Although the state cannot directly ensure that no one is lonely, it is possible to help in making it easy to meet other people (support transport for the elderly, support leisure activities, etc.). Therefore, even if the state might not be able to counteract the fact that some do not feel they have a good life, it might frame options and possibilities for doing something about the issue by changing the context people are living in.

Table 3.1 is also an example that well-being and understanding of the development herein includes people's happiness. Again, what makes the individual happy can be, and is, very different. The state cannot guarantee happiness, and it cannot decide what is the best way to live in order to have a happy life, but it might help in setting the scene for the fact that it can be possible to live a fulfilling life. So the state can help in ensuring options and context for the individual to pursue a life which also, in a subjective sense, is good.

An example of this is by trying to reduce the risk of unemployment; see also Chapter 7. This is due to the very negative impact of unemployment on people's well-being. It has been argued that there are three types of loss connected to losing a job: "loss of agency, loss of the functions of paid work; and loss of social status" (Sage, 2017, p. 1) or, more simply, "income, control, autonomy, status, respect, dignity, structure and skills" (p. 6). Sage also refers to a central explanation being, with reference to Jahoda, that it causes latent deprivation.

Furthermore, this also points to the fact that the understanding of well-being and welfare can be, and is, different for individuals. Still, at a societal level, it is important to have a grasp of what they are as this gives guidelines as to how to proceed with social policy in such a way that it increases the quality of life for as many individuals as possible.

Welfare can be defined as: "the highest possible access to economic resources, a high level of well-being, including the happiness of the citizens, a guaranteed minimum income to avoid living in poverty, and, finally, having the capabilities to ensure the individual a good life" (Greve, 2008, p. 50).

As with all definitions, the previous definition does not necessarily imply that it is possible to say what instruments can be used to achieve the aims, it merely indicates what important issues are at stake. Thus, as an example, a high level of well-being is, as argued previously, not necessarily easy to measure in an objective way. A guaranteed minimum income to avoid living in poverty depends on the definition of poverty used in the country (see later discussion on the measurement of poverty, in Section 3.5). For some, in order to enhance well-being, it will not be sufficient to avoid living in poverty, it will also be central to live at the same level as persons they compare themselves with, i.e. the relative position is important (Ejrnæs and Greve, 2017).

## 3.3.  OLD AND NEW SOCIAL RISKS

Historically, as also described in previous chapters, social policy was mainly about income transfers for unemployment, sickness, work injury and becoming old. There was some health care and hospital treatment as a service aspect, albeit the central issue was how to ensure that people in case a contingency occurred in one of these four central areas, thus needing at least some income transfers, were provided with a benefit. This is because, in the wake of industrialisation, previous support in these cases was taken care of by civil society. The size of the benefits was not large from the beginning.

Much later, benefits were extended in many countries to include various family benefits and supports to cover housing costs for low-income earners. Family benefits and family policy can thus be seen as a late part of the social policy development in many countries.

When there was a need to cover these contingencies, what we now label "old risk", this was gradually done in most western countries. Societies develop and new types of risk emerge. New risks are defined as "the risks that people now face in the course of their lives as a result of the economic and social changes associated with the transition to a post-industrial society" (Taylor-Gooby, 2004, p. 2).

The reason for the new risks is related to the higher level of women having a job, the increasing pressure on the labour market, break-ups in families and, further, the need to balance work and family life.

The new social risks are thus not only concerned with income transfers and social benefits, but also different kinds of services. Services that by themselves can improve well-being and quality of life for the individual, but might also have a positive impact on relatives/friends. Examples of services can be day care for children (to enable both partners to be on the labour market), upgrading and upskilling to ensure a continuous ability to have a job, or care for the frail elderly (to enable partner or children to stay on the labour market). Thereby, social policy is no longer just an issue of income transfers to those who, for one reason or another, are outside the labour market, but also different kinds of services making and improving well-being for citizens. Care for children, for example, has been extended in many countries in recent years.

Coverage and support to cope with new social risks is, however, not only an issue related to services. Gradually, in many countries, there has also been a development with different kinds of leave (maternity, paternity and/or parental) in order to make it possible for children to get a good start in life, but also so that various kinds of leave can be both a substitute or supplement to the delivery of child care.

Several new types of social risk are not only an issue for state policy, they are also an issue for the labour market, in the sense that, for example, the ability to combine work and family life also depends on how flexible workplaces are with regard to number of hours of work, when being able to leave the workplace (e.g. in case of sickness of a child) and what time to start and finish. Ensuring the necessary skills for the workforce can also be argued to be part of the responsibilities of companies. Part of this can be labelled occupational welfare (Farnsworth, 2018); see also Chapter 2.

Last, civil society still has a role here, for example, in that the extended family also helps in caring for children or a frail relative (which, for example, can be people with disabilities or elderly persons).

It is difficult to be very precise as to whether or not what is labelled new social risk has caused a pressure on old social risk, as the size and spending on social policy also relates to how rich a society is; see also Chapter 4. Given societies over the last 100 years have become richer, this has opened up the way for more spending in the field of social policy, albeit still with strong differences among countries.

## 3.4. INSTRUMENTS AND WELL-BEING

Well-being is described in Section 3.2. However, this does not, in itself, point to what kind of instruments in social policy need to be used if one wants to increase the well-being of citizens.

Starting from the basic needs, this will imply that society is able to help those not able to do so by themselves by providing at least a place to live, and income in such a way they can have food. So, food and shelter could be the first issue to be covered. This is largely in line with coverage of old social risk. The way in which support to housing could be done can vary, but in one way or another housing is, as it also was in the Beveridge report, a central instrument that can be supported directly by public welfare or indirectly by fiscal welfare, or sometimes labelled tax-expenditure (Sinfield, 2018); see also Chapter 2.

What is seen as necessary for living can vary between countries, and can also depend on the more normative stance of how well people dependent on public income transfers should live. Still, a variation of income transfers can be understood as an important part of ensuring and improving well-being for citizens.

We know that being at risk of becoming unemployed or being unemployed can have a strong negative impact on the well-being of an individual (and often also the spouse/partner and children), so policies that can help people back to the labour market (see also Chapter 6) can be an important issue for welfare states if the aim is to increase the well-being of citizens. It is also important that the replacement rate is relatively high, as this reduces the economic anxiety of becoming unemployed, although it is not sufficient to reduce the negative impact on well-being of losing one's job.

Making it possible to combine work and family life will also be an issue that is important in order to increase well-being. This is also because the level of happiness for people looks like a u-curve, so that people are happier when young and old, and less happy when they are in the middle of their life. Part of the reason for this is that in mid-life it can often be difficult to get work and family life to fit together, but might naturally also be because people are disappointed in what they have been able to achieve so far.

Countries have different policies with regard to both income transfers and services to people with disabilities. Compared to other areas, benefits and services to people with disabilities are often without means-testing, as the services and benefits are aimed at making it possible for people with disabilities to live a life as close as possible to people without disabilities. Disability policy is also an example of an area where what is not classical social policy can have an impact on daily life, for example, by making it possible to enter buildings and make infrastructure accessible.

Care for the frail elderly, including long-term care, has moved higher on the agenda in recent years due to demographic changes and the increasing number of elderly. Countries provide long-term care in very different ways, with some mainly relying on the family, some having a focus on marketisation and some with more state involvement; see Greve (2017). Furthermore, this is a service where the boundaries between care at hospitals and long-term care might be blurred, and therefore data on spending and activities within the area are not always precise.

Social integration, for example reducing loneliness among the elderly, but also integration in the wider context of migrants and refugees, has also moved higher on the agenda in many countries. For migrants, this often revolves around integration on the labour market; see more in Chapters 6 and 7.

Naturally, there are also policies outside the classical social policy area that can be important (health, environment, etc.), but this is outside the scope of this book.

Overall, this points to the fact that when and if wanting to do something for people's well-being, social policy has a role, especially in relation to everyday life, including to alleviate poverty. In order to alleviate poverty, one needs to know how this can be defined and measured, and this is discussed in Section 3.5.

## 3.5. POVERTY AND INEQUALITY

Poverty and inequality are seen as central issues in relation to well-being. This is because when living in poverty, an individual might not be able to get his/her basic needs fulfilled, whereas a high level of inequality also reduces the option for the achievement of well-being for some.

The level of poverty and inequality can be measured in many and varied ways. Nevertheless, before measuring it, one needs to define the concept. Eurostat's definition is shown in Box 3.1.

### BOX 3.1   AT RISK OF POVERTY – WHAT DOES IT MEAN?

The at-risk-of-poverty rate is the share of people with an equivalised disposable income (after social transfer) below the at-risk-of-poverty threshold, which is set at 60 % of the national median equivalised disposable income after social transfers.

This indicator does not measure wealth or poverty, but low income in comparison to other residents in that country, which does not necessarily imply a low standard of living.

The at-risk-of-poverty rate before social transfers is calculated as the share of people having an equivalised disposable income before social transfers that is below the at-risk-of-poverty threshold calculated after social transfers. Pensions, such as old-age and survivors' (widows' and widowers') benefits, are counted as income (before social transfers) and not as social transfers. This indicator examines the hypothetical non-existence of social transfers.

The persistent at-risk-of-poverty rate shows the percentage of the population living in households where the equivalised disposable income was below the at-risk-of-poverty threshold for the current year and at least two out of the preceding three years. Its calculation requires a longitudinal instrument, through which the individuals are followed over four years.

Source: http://ec.europa.eu/eurostat/statistics-explained/index.php/ Glossary:At-risk-of-poverty_rate, accessed the 12th of May, 2017.

Eurostat defines relative poverty as the number of people having an income below 60% of median income. Equivalisation of income refers to the fact that it takes into account the number of people in the household, which is done by counting one for the first adult; 0.5 for the second and each subsequent person aged 14 and over; and, last, 0.3 for each child aged under 14. This reflects the fact that it is more expensive to live alone than together with other family members, where you can share rent and insurance, and it is often cheaper to buy and make food for more than one person at a time. The disposable income refers to the fact that the impact of the income tax system is taken into account (but not the value-added taxes), and it can be before and after social transfers from the welfare state. The best instrument is when social transfers are taken into consideration, as this better reflects what the person has access to. Further, the difference in the number of people living in poverty before and after social transfers might be argued to inform about the effectiveness of the welfare state in alleviating poverty, given the level of spending on social security.

Table 3.2 shows the percentage of people in the EU28 at risk of poverty depending on the threshold used.

As Table 3.2 shows, the lower the threshold, the fewer people are said to live at risk of poverty. Eurostat often uses the 60% level. The same threshold is only used when defining if a person is working poor, e.g. despite having a job the person is not able to have a disposable income above the poverty level (see further later).

The reason for labelling it "at risk" of poverty is that the persons might have other assets not counted as income, and they

*Table* 3.2   Threshold percentages and numbers of people at risk of poverty in 2015 in EU28 dependent on threshold used

| EU28 | 2015 |
|------|------|
| 40% | 6.3 |
| 50% | 10.8 |
| 60% | 17.3 |
| 70% | 25.0 |

Source: Eurostat, ilc_lio2, accessed the 12th of May, 2017

might be supported by family or friends or have low costs, for example, in relation to housing. Furthermore, it might be one year with a low income (a person starting a new company, a student or a person just retired), and therefore one is also trying to calculate the risk of persistent living in poverty. This is defined as three consecutive years with an income below the set level; see Box 3.1.

Social policy can help to alleviate poverty by providing services or through income transfers. The level of the benefits and criteria for getting these benefits varies across countries. This can be due to differences in economic options, but also ideological preferences might influence the decisions. Therefore, in some systems benefits are paid out in kind, and not in cash, as some are willing to pay for food, but not for income transfers which can be used for other purposes; see also Chapter 4 on legitimacy.

A central concept is also the working poor, which is defined as those who are in work, but have an equivalised income below the 60% median level of income. In the EU28, around one in every ten people are working poor. This is an indicator that even getting a job might not help in alleviating poverty, due to low income, only being able to get a part-time job or working as self-employed; see also Chapter 6 on the labour market. Working poor can also be seen as a new social risk. Lower taxes or in-work tax credits is in some countries an approach used in order to increase disposable income. However, at the same time, this implies that those not having a job, who do not get this tax-reduction, will be seen as having a relatively lower level of disposable income.

Poverty can be understood as a multidimensional problem, despite the fact that it is frequently (and still mainly) measured in monetary terms (as described previously). Instead, there might be a need for having a multidimensional poverty index (Alkire and Santos, 2013), which also focuses on other aspects – for example, access to welfare services and, in some countries, clean water, housing or nutrition, etc.

The issues about a broader understanding also reflect why one needs to include other aspects when looking into the well-being of people, as this also not only depends on whether or not one is living in poverty, albeit there is a connection. Poverty and well-being can both depend on material deprivation.

The definition of material deprivation is shown in Box 3.2.

---

**BOX 3.2 EU'S DEFINITION OF MATERIAL DEPRIVATION**

The severe material deprivation rate represents the proportion of people living in households that cannot afford at least four of the following nine items:

- mortgage or rent payments, utility bills, hire purchase instalments or other loan payments;
- one week's holiday away from home;
- a meal with meat, chicken, fish or vegetarian equivalent every second day;
- unexpected financial expenses;
- a telephone (including mobile telephone);
- a colour TV;
- a washing machine;
- a car; and
- heating to keep the home adequately warm.

Source: http://ec.europa.eu/eurostat/statistics-explained/index.php/Material_deprivation_statistics_-_early_results, accessed the 12th of May, 2017.

---

In 2016, around 8% of EU citizens had severe material deprivation using the rule of not being able to afford at least four of the nine of the indicators shown previously. There can always be a discussion as to what the correct items are that can be seen as relating to being deprived and whether they are necessary items. However, using such a metric opens the way for the possibilities of having knowledge about development, and also indicating important issues related to well-being. Thereby, also that social policy could aim to ensure that severe material deprivation does not take place.

The change in equality and the possible consequences hereof has come under increasing discussion in recent years (Piketty, 2014; Stiglitz, 2012; Atkinson, 2014; Atkinson, 2015; Reich, 2015). This is not the place to present the many and varied viewpoints in this debate, but more to reflect upon how we can measure and understand the concept of equality. This also as a consequence of the fact that inequality has been increasing in recent years in many countries, often due to a combination of retrenchment, lower taxes of high-income earners and an increase in capital income for those with the highest wealth who are often taxed at a very low level. Social policy (and economic policy) has thereby, in many countries, had a less redistributive role than previously.

The fact that there are differences between countries is shown in Figure 3.2, which shows the inequality in EU-member states in 2016 (or the latest available year), from close to 40 in Bulgaria, to less than 25 in Slovakia.

The fact that inequality has detrimental effects has been shown in several studies, from having more crime, less trust and several other problems compared to more equal societies (Wilkinson and Pickett, 2009), to a possible negative impact on growth (IMF, 2015).

New theoretical approaches also point to the fact that the elimination of poverty cannot only be achieved by strong work-incentives and influences on individuals' behaviour, but instead there is a need also to look into the way the social safety net functions (Curchin, 2017).

## 3.6. IS IT THE SAME IN ALL WELFARE STATES?

Naturally, social policy is not the same in all welfare states. There is only place for some more general remarks and classifications

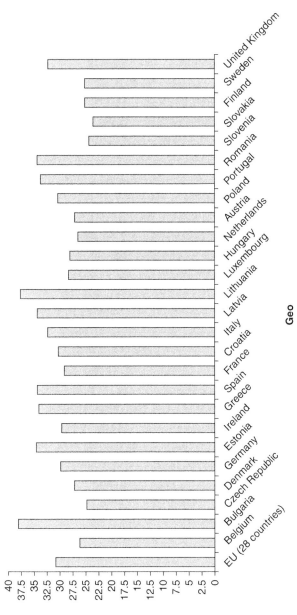

*Figure 3.2* Gini-coefficient in EU countries 2016
Source: Eurostat, tessi190, accessed the 6th of July, 2017

here. For an overview of European individual countries, see Schubert, Villota and Kuhlmann (2016); and for an updated and detailed description of many different welfare regimes around the world, see Greve (2018). Here just a few words to indicate the differences. The classical welfare regimes are the Nordic (seen as universal, high level of benefits, general, high degree of equality and encompassing), the continental (occupational based, middle level of benefits, some degree of universality and equality) and the liberal (market based, universal, low level of benefits, less degree of equality). Eastern European countries and Southern European countries have variations and differences, whereas the US, Australia, Canada and New Zealand often are characterised as liberal welfare states.

Following this, spending can briefly be summed up, by that the situation is as follows. The Nordic welfare states in Europe often spend more on welfare policies than is spent by the continental countries in Europe, albeit France also has a high level of spending. The liberal welfare states (such as the UK and the US) spend to a more limited extent on social policy, and this is also the case for many southern and eastern European countries. The reasons for the lower level of spending can, however, be different and have different kinds of arguments – for example, the reason might be more ideological in some countries and lack of funds in other countries.

As can be seen from the Table 3.3, social protection varies from just over 12% of GDP to more than 34% – so there is a large variety among countries. However, the percentages are not comparable as in some countries income transfers are taxable income, whereas this is not the case in others. Still, there are large variations in the social policy effort.

Different countries might also vary the field where they spend money. A certain kind of path-dependency might be the case if, for example, there was an initial strong focus on old age then it might be difficult to transfer money to other areas. There will also (see more in Chapter 5) be an impact from ideas, including different opinions on the balance especially between state and market.

Not only is social policy different in various countries; the level of well-being also varies, with the Nordic countries often

*Table 3.3* Social protection spending as percentages of GDP in 2015 or nearest year

| Geo/time | 2015 |
| --- | --- |
| European Union (28 countries) | 28.7 |
| Belgium | 30.3 |
| Bulgaria | 18.5 |
| Czech Republic | 19.1 |
| Denmark | 32.9 |
| Germany | 29.1 |
| Estonia | 15.1 |
| Ireland | 20.6 |
| Greece | 26.0 |
| Spain | 24.7 |
| France | 33.9 |
| Croatia | 21.3 |
| Italy | 30.0 |
| Cyprus | 23.0 |
| Latvia | 14.9 |
| Lithuania | 15.6 |
| Luxembourg | 22.0 |
| Hungary | 19.9 |
| Malta | 18.2 |
| Netherlands | 30.9 |
| Austria | 30.0 |
| Poland | 19.1 |
| Portugal | 26.9 |
| Romania | 14.8 |
| Slovenia | 24.1 |
| Slovakia | 18.3 |
| Finland | 31.9 |
| Sweden | 29.3 |
| United Kingdom | 27.4 |

Source: Eurostat spr_exp_sum, accessed the 22nd of September, 2017

being among those happiest, together with countries such as the Netherlands, Canada, Switzerland, Australia and New Zealand. Important issues for this can be social support, trust and income, which are all aspects that have an impact (Helliwell, Layard and Sachs, 2017). In this way social policy by, for example, helping to reduce the number of people being lonely can be a way of improving well-being in countries. The degree of social cohesion is also an important marker of well-being. This points to the fact that social policy is not only about money, but also about how to help in relationships, trust in other people and in general social inclusion in societies.

If one wants to have detailed knowledge on individual countries, one might naturally look into national reports and information. However, this can make it difficult to make comparisons with the situation in other countries. Therefore, good sources to use when comparing are as follows. For Europe: Eurostat and various reports from the European Commission. For the developed countries: OECD. For the rest of the world: international organisations such as the IMF (International Monetary Fund), the UN (United Nations), the ILO (International Labour Organization) and the WHO (World Health Organization).

## 3.7. SUMMING UP

Social policy is not the same across countries, including differences in how much money is spent on welfare and on what types of social policy there are and how generous the benefits are. However, there are some common elements and discussions in most countries. These are discussions revolving around the level of benefits, who is eligible for benefits and under what conditions. Behind this is often an (albeit mainly implicit) understanding of who is deserving and who is not deserving of different types of social benefits.

All countries also have some degree of inequality and some people living in poverty, or as labelled in the EU, at risk of poverty. There are issues and difficulties in measuring both poverty and inequality; however, if measuring it in the same way over time and across countries, it informs about the difference, development and levels hereof. Whether one, as a consequence of the level of poverty or inequality, would make a public sector intervention and decide new social policy issues is, at the end of the day, a political decision. Recent years have seen an increase in inequality and poverty in many countries. The generosity of income transfers can be an important element in the size and degree of inequality, but also the way the tax system influences the level of inequality. In-work poverty, or working poor, is an issue that has increased in recent years.

There are old and there are new social risks – and this will, presumably, continue to be the case. Old risk relates to four classical aspects: old age, sickness, unemployment and work injury. The distinction is perhaps not in itself important in order to understand social policy, but it is important as a way of being able to grasp how new types of systems develop, what kind of needs might arise and that there can be a need for state intervention in order to support different groups of people. The work–family life balance is an example of an important new social risk. This as most people in the working age would like to have a job, but they would also like to have a family, including children. If, for example, there are not day-care institutions or they are very expensive, this might make it difficult to combine this.

Looking at well-being is perhaps also not a new issue; however, recent years have seen a growing interest in well-being and happiness as a way to inform about the quality of life, and thereby also pointing to the fact that money is not everything, although those countries having more money are also able to spend more on social policy; cf. also Chapter 4.

Well-being is, like the measurement of poverty and inequality, a many-faceted issue. However, it seems to be important to achieve at least a certain degree of equality, and also to have social policy that, at least to a certain extent, ensures and tries to reduce the level of poverty. It can also be services helping the individual to be able to have a good life, such as health – or long-term care.

## REFERENCES

Adler, A. and Seligman, M. (2016), Using Wellbeing for Public Policy: Theory, Measurement, and Recommendations. *International Journal of Wellbeing*, vol. 6, no. 1, pp. 1–35.

Alkire, S. and Santos, M. (2013), A Multidimensional Approach: Poverty Measurement & Beyond. *Social Indicator Research*, vol. 112, pp. 239–257.

Allardt, E. (1993), *Having, Loving, Being: An Alternative to the Swedish Model of Welfare Research in Nussbaum, M. and Sen, A.: The Quality of Life*. Oxford, Clarendon Paperbacks.

Atkinson, A. B. (2014), After Piketty. *British Journal of Sociology*, vol. 65, no. 4, pp. 619–638.

Atkinson, A. B. (2015), *Inequality: What Can Be Done*. Cambridge, Harvard University Press.

Curchin, K. (2017), Using Behavioural Insights to Argue for a Stronger Social Safety Net: Beyond Libertarian Paternalism. *Journal of Social Policy*, vol. 46, no. 2, pp. 231–249.

Dabla-Norris, E. et al. (2015), Causes and Consequences of Income Inequality: A Global Perspective. IMF Staff Discussion Note, SDN/15/13, IMF.

Ejrnæs, A. and Greve, B. (2017), Your Position in Society Matters for How Happy You Are. *International Journal of Social Welfare*, vol. 26, no. 3, pp. 206–217. doi: 10.1111/ijsw.12233.

Farnsworth, K. (2018), Occupational Welfare in Greve, B. ed., *The Routledge Handbook of the Welfare State*, 2nd edition. Oxon, Routledge.

Greve, B. (2008), What Is Welfare? *Central European Journal of Public Policy*, vol. 2, no. 1, pp. 50–73.

Greve, B. (2017), How to Measure Social Progress, *Social Policy & Administration*, vol. 51. vol. 7, pp. 1002–1022.

Greve, B. ed. (2018), *The Routledge Handbook of the Welfare State*, 2nd edition. Oxon, Routledge.

Helliwell, J., Layard, R. and Sachs, J. (2017), *World Happiness Report, 2017*. http://worldhappiness.report/ed/2017/.

Maslow, A. H. (1943), A Theory of Human Motivation. *Psychological Review*, vol. 50, no. 4, pp. 370–396.

Piketty, T. (2014), *Capital in the Twenty-First Century*. Cambridge, The Belknap Press of Harvard University Press.

Reich, R. (2015), *Saving Capitalism: For the Many, Not the Few*. New York, Alfred A. Knopf.

Sage, D. (2017), Reversing the Negative Experience of Unemployment: A Mediating Role for Social Policies. *Social Policy & Administration*, pre-publication.

Schubert, K., Villota, P. and Kuhlmann, J. (2016), *Challenges to European Welfare Systems*. Heidelberg, Springer.

Sinfield, A. (2018), Fiscal Welfare in Greve, B. ed., *The Routledge Handbook of the Welfare State*, 2nd edition. Oxon, Routledge.

Stiglitz, J. (2012), *The Price of Inequality*. London, W.W. Norton & Company.

Taylor-Gooby, P. ed. (2004) *New Risks, New Welfare: The Transformation of the European Welfare State*. Oxford, Oxford University Press.

Wilkinson, R. and Pickett, K. (2009), *The Spirit Level: Why Greater Equality Makes Societies Stronger*. London, Bloomsbury Press.

# CRISIS AND NEW WAYS IN WELFARE STATES

## 4.1. INTRODUCTION

Welfare states have been argued to be in crisis for many years (OECD, 1981 as an early example). The arguments and reasons, therefore, have been different and have varied over time and across countries. A lack of legitimacy for many reasons in the different welfare states has been one issue. Another is the lack of financial means to develop and enhance social and labour policy for the variety of needs and changing needs over time. How to choose what type of instruments to use and implement, and with the best results, has therefore become increasingly more important.

This chapter therefore probes into how to evaluate social policy, how to understand evaluation in the field, and also discusses the use and misuse of social policy evaluation, including how evaluation can be used as a way of developing effective social policy. This also as recent years have seen a surge and focus on how to best achieve the aim of social policy, given the pressure on welfare states' ability to finance social policy. Thus, there has been an increased focus on what does and does not work, for example the movement towards evidence-based social policy.

This is further also a consequence that different approaches can have different impacts on users. However, the chapter starts with a short description of the most recent crisis and the possible cause for crisis in welfare states, then proceeds with a discussion of the legitimacy of social policy, and then touches upon how to finance welfare states, before turning to the issue of evaluation.

## 4.2. WHY CRISIS?

There are many and varied issues at stake in order to explain the crisis of the welfare states. The crisis has been argued to be due to the fact that welfare states did not reach their goals of redistribution, lacked administrative efficiency and were an economic burden on societies' development due to the possible distortion of taxes and duties (this is investigated in Section 4.3). Whether taxes and duties have a negative impact can be discussed, as this needs to be measured against what one gets for the money; see also social investment in Chapter 5.

Naturally, one can question what a crisis is. This can be seen as a time which profoundly changes institutions, structure and/or systems; what in Hall's understanding is a critical juncture (Hall, 1993). This might also across countries cause a convergence in policies, understanding and interpretations of what the welfare state's role is. However, for the purpose here, a crisis is when welfare states are not sustainable – understood either as a lack of legitimacy and/or financing.

The increase in the number of elderly relative to those on the labour market has also caused concerns, and for example, has been a reason for pension reforms in many countries by postponing the age when one can get state pension, and changing the calculation of benefit given longer life expectancy (Hinrichs, 2018). It is the case that not only pensioners are outside the labour market, as this quote shows for the EU:

> Last year, 89 million people aged 15 to 64 were economically inactive in the European Union (EU). In other words, slightly more than a quarter (27.1%) of the EU population aged 15–64 stood outside the labour market, being neither employed nor unemployed. This included people who were in education or training (35% of the inactive people),

retired (16%), suffering from serious illness or disability (16%), or also those who were looking after children or incapacitated adults (10%). Women made up the majority of this economically active population group (60%). In total, almost 8 in 10 inactive people (78%) declared that they did not wish to work.[1]

So, one challenge in relation to this is the combination of expenditures on social policy and possible issues in how to finance the welfare state; see also Section 4.4.

The focus in this section is albeit more on the consequences of the last financial crisis. Starting in 2008 in the US with the collapse of financial institutions, this spread quickly to the rest of the world and especially Europe, where many banks also got into difficulties, and whereby many countries were forced to bail out these banks. This caused an increase in unemployment, lower income from taxes and duties (due to the lower economic activity) and a higher public sector deficit. This also caused a growing public sector debt that some countries had stark difficulties in financing at a reasonable interest rate. Debt and deficit were higher than the Maastricht criteria (3% of GDP in deficit, 0.5% in structural deficit and a maximum of 60% of GDP in debt), which most EU countries (all those having a euro currency) are obliged to follow. Ireland, for example, had a deficit of more than 30% of GDP; see also Figure 4.1.

Thus, the bailout of banks caused increasing deficits and debts, making it difficult to finance social policy. It was at the same time a period where the housing bubble burst, partly due to very high and inflated prices, partly as a consequence of more people being unable to pay their mortgages. The financial crisis influenced not only public sector deficit and debt, but also caused negative economic growth and increased unemployment levels. Austerity policies were enacted in many countries, with a reduction in spending as a consequence of the fact that liberal ideas (see Chapter 5) had an influence on the policy recommendations.

Due to economic globalisation, crisis today has a faster and quicker impact in many countries, while at the same time, globalisation opens the way for better options for trade.

Thus, the crisis has had many and varied reasons – one being the legitimacy of social policy, as investigated in Section 4.3.

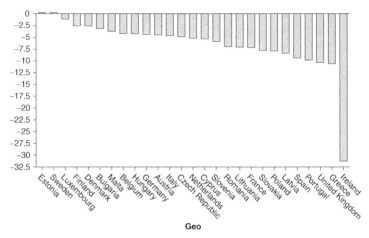

*Figure 4.1*    Public deficit as proportion of GDP in 2010
Source: Eurostat

## 4.3. LEGITIMACY OF SOCIAL POLICY

Why have an interest in the legitimacy of social policy, one could ask? Is this not just a matter of whether there is a political majority willing and prepared to pay for social policy, so that the median voter is important? However, the legitimacy of the policy can have an influence on what type of social policy is enacted and, further, who gets what kind of benefit, and whether the population is willing to pay for welfare.

Historically, one type of legitimacy has revolved around the fact that there was redistribution over the life course (see Yerkes and Peper, 2018), so that if one generation paid for old-age pension, care for the elderly, etc., then the next generation would also pay when the present generation becomes old. At the same time, it was related to the fact that there was support when one is growing up; one pays when on the labour market; and one receives while no longer able to be on the labour market. In this sense, part of the legitimacy of the welfare state revolves around self-interest (Blekesaune and Quadagno, 2003), and thereby giving higher support for social policy in areas where people might expect themselves or someone close to themselves to have an interest. Besides that, there can also be support due to social norms (Roosma, Oorschot and Gelissen, 2016).

This further reflects another issue of legitimacy that benefits should go to those who are deserving and not to those who are undeserving, or at least seen by the majority as undeserving. The understanding of who deserves and who does not has changed over time. Thus, in general it seems in most countries, that groups who actively, or over the majority of their life, try to and have been able to support themselves are perceived to be more deserving than those who do not. Those who are grateful for support are also more deserving than others, and the more we know those in need, the more they might be seen as more deserving (identity). Support for the welfare state might also vary across different groups (e.g. high/low income, men/women, old/young, native/non-native, big cities/country).

Support might change over time, for example, so that in times of high levels of unemployment there might be more willingness to support people economically without a job, when it does not look like people can find a job, and when many know someone without a job, who is perhaps desperate to get a job. Deservingness has been argued to have five dimensions, which also sums up the previous arguments (Oorschot, 2008):

a) Control
b) Need
c) Identity
d) Attitude
e) Reciprocity

Over time, especially, those who reach the age of retirement are, in most countries, seen as deserving as they have contributed over their lifetime to society by working and by taking care of children and sometimes also their own parents. Pensions are therefore also a policy that people support, and in general so that "the needs of old age have traditionally topped the list of deserving areas of social provision" (Taylor-Gooby, 2017, p. 826. People with disabilities are often also seen as a group who are in clear need of support from the welfare state.

In contrast to this, those on social assistance and unemployment benefits have often had less support from the public, in fact, often without the public actually knowing the size of the benefit, but believing that the level of benefit is very high and given to some people who do not really "contribute" to society's development.

Table 4.1 shows the issues related to the perceptions of the mistargeting of benefits.

The knowledge on who uses (under or over) the welfare state can influence the perceptions and thereby the legitimacy of the welfare state. This thus can be due both to low take-up rates (e.g. this shows the proportion of eligible people who actually get the benefit) and the level of benefits. Information on the level of take-up rates is very limited, and it seems that only the UK produces official estimates hereof (Roosma, Oorschot and Gelissen, 2016). Related to legitimacy, the issue is then the perception that if many people get a benefit (overuse) for any reason, this will reduce support for the welfare states. Knowledge among the public of the actual size of benefit is often also not very high.

Migrants and people using the right to free movement of workers in the EU are often also portrayed as less deserving, with the understanding that they should be supported in their homeland. This is a more difficult issue to address, and whether migrants, not only in Europe, and free movement cause "social tourism" might depend on how one measures the short- and long-term impact of migration. In the short term, those coming to a country and having a job will contribute to production and

*Table 4.1* Perceptions of underuse and overuse of benefits

|  | Underuse | Overuse |
|---|---|---|
| Intended | So low levels of benefits or strong stigma attached that people do not search, or difficult administrative procedures | Reflects that if individual gets a benefit they should not have had (fraud or abuse) |
| Unintended | People do not receive benefits they are eligible to | People not seen as deserving receiving benefits |

Source: Inspired by Roosma, Oorschot and Gelissen (2016)

pay taxes and duties, and this can therefore also in the long term have a positive economic impact of migration on the countries receiving migrants. However, if migrants are eligible for social benefits (such as family/child allowances), this might be deemed as unfair by some, especially if they are also seen as a threat to people's own jobs (see also Chapter 6), and on the level of wages through different kinds of social dumping.

This is also reflected in what has been labelled "welfare chauvinism", defined as "a political view that promotes nativism as the main organizing principle of social policy" (Ennser-Jedenastik, 2017, p. 3). By "nativism" it is meant that benefits should mainly be to the native population, and not to migrants or others who have come to a country, unless they have contributed to the welfare system. It is therefore also argued that welfare chauvinism will be higher for universal or means-tested benefits, in contrast to social insurance. This is because in social insurance the individual is expected to have paid into the system. The increase in welfare chauvinism can be interpreted as a reduced legitimacy in welfare states, at least related to some of the benefits, whereas aspects such as health care and pensions has to a lesser degree been questioned.

In relation to legitimacy, another issue is the size of benefit and the conditions attached to receiving it. It seems that if one wants to reduce poverty, it is not enough to do so with tough sanctions, and with the expectation of reciprocity, attitude and identity, as argued previously, but also that a good safety net will be a core issue if one is enabled to reduce poverty and inequality (Curchin, 2017). However, the willingness to pay a high level of benefits can be dependent on the understanding of whether people might themselves, at some time, be in need, and also who is going to pay for the benefits. Thus, the financing of social policy can also influence its legitimacy (Morel and Palme, 2018).

## 4.4. ABILITIES TO FINANCE WELFARE

The abilities to finance welfare depend overall on the size of the welfare states and the willingness among decision makers to claim taxes and duties to pay for welfare, and the efficiency of the tax administration, including the level of the hidden economy.

A tax is defined as a payment without any guaranteed return. So, just because one has paid income tax or, for example, VAT (value-added tax), one has no right to receive social benefits. This is in contrast to insurance (although see social insurance later), where one gets a payment if a social contingency occurs, and it is also different to payments into pension funds, where the individual gets back in proportion relative to what he/she has paid into the pension fund.

There is a link between the size of the welfare state and the need for taxes and duties. This, however, has some caveats. First, the social and labour market policy might also be paid for by companies through occupational welfare (see Chapter 2 and Farnsworth, 2018); second, there can also be private savings or obligatory social insurance that can finance social policy. If the social insurances are obligatory, then this resembles traditional income taxation, and is understood in statistics as a way to finance welfare in different countries. For the individual, the differences are also marginal, as in both cases, it has an impact on the disposable income the individual has in order to pay for daily life. If it is voluntary social insurance, which exists even in universal welfare states, then access to welfare depends on the individual's ability and willingness to pay for the insurance and be able to fulfil the conditions for receiving the benefit. Therefore, voluntary insurances tend to have a negative impact on distribution. It is especially in relation to unemployment benefit, pension and health care that there is the use of insurance.

Third, welfare services might also be paid for by users by different kinds of user charges. They might cover all costs, but might also be at a lower level so that the payment only covers part of the cost of the service. The argument for user charges is that they help in informing on the individual's preference or need for the specific service. For example, this has been the argument for introducing a fee for visiting a general practitioner. Payment for at least part of the cost of medicine is also a user charge. The impact of user charges on the individual's well-being depends not only on the size of the user charge, but also on the level of income and/or social income transfers the individual has, including his/her possible wealth. However, the overall impact is often argued to influence negatively on the distribution of consumption possibilities, as the cost of the users are relatively more burdensome for low-income earners than for high-income earners. High levels of user charges might thus, for example, reduce the option for all families with children to use day care, thus making it more difficult for some families than for other families to combine work and family life.

Fourth, in some countries, part of social policy is paid for by altruistic and voluntary support, which is albeit only a more limited part of social policy financing in those countries. A risk hereby is further that it is not decided democratically who can be supported and who cannot be supported, but will depend on the preference of those donating money. Furthermore, this might not be a stable way of financing given that when being voluntary it can also be stopped from one day to another.

Fifth, in case of economic crisis benefits can, for a short while, be paid for by public sector deficit, albeit not all the time, and if there is a large public sector debt, this might need to be paid by future generations. A high public sector debt might also make it more difficult for a country to finance the debt, with the risk that high interest rates can reduce the options to finance social policy in the years to come.

As in other social policy issues and aspects, each means of financing welfare has both pro and con arguments. This can only to a more limited extent be presented here; see instead, Barr (2012). However, a few core aspects can be pointed out. They reflect mainly the impact on distribution and saving, and the balance between work and leisure.

In the case of voluntary insurance, the risk is that for some it will be too expensive to be covered by insurance if they have a high risk of disease, are in a profession with a high degree of unemployment or in a type of job with a high risk of work accidents. There might also be a risk that people underestimate their need for support, and/or constantly postpone decisions on taking up insurance. So, voluntary insurance has a high risk of causing inequality in access to coverage both in relation to old and new social risks, and might also cause higher state expenditure for hospitals if there is universal access to these when in acute need of care, which is the case in most welfare systems.

Implementation of user charges can have the same impact as argued previously, although if they are reduced or not in place at all for low-income families, the possible negative impact on distribution will be reduced.

Different taxes and duties have different impacts, which are dependent on the precise way they have been enacted. Income tax can be regressive, proportional and progressive, implying that the impact on distribution depends upon how each country has endorsed and developed its own tax system. If regressive, low-income earners pay a relatively higher proportion; if proportional, it is the same relative share; and if progressive, the tax system is argued to have a Robin Hood effect. Income taxes are also argued to change the balance between work and leisure, albeit this can both be towards more leisure or more work – and it is difficult to estimate the precise size of the impact.

Duties tend to have an upside-down effect because low-income earners will have to spend a larger proportion of their income on consumption than high-income earners. However, for some luxury goods, it might be possible to ensure a more equal balance by looking into what different groups in society consume.

At the same time, this reflects a dilemma in social policy as some duties, for example, might be decided in order to reduce smoking and alcohol consumption, in order to improve health, albeit this might negatively influence opportunities for low-income households. In the increasingly global world, it is difficult to have widely varying levels of duty in these areas in neighbouring countries because if the duties are too high, many people will travel and buy the goods cheaper close by.

The impact of globalisation on financing is also obvious – in many countries, taxes on companies' profits have been reduced as a way of attracting companies into countries, and tax havens are used in order to reduce the tax to be paid. So, countries might not pursue exactly the balance they would prefer.

It is in this balancing act that decisions on the levels and structures of taxes, duties and user charges need to find a balance. This is further influenced by the idea of how, and to what large degree, society should help in alleviating poverty and increasing equality due to different ideas in social policy; see also Chapter 5.

Last, the ability to finance social policy also depends on how rich a country is. This is shown in Figure 4.2, for all EU28 member states' GDP and spending on social policy in euros per head.

As the figure indicates, among the EU-member states there is a clear connection between how rich a country is and how large social spending is. The implication being that, in many countries, the overall economic position will also have an impact on how large a welfare state there is.

One could argue that it is the relative spending that is important. This is shown in Figure 4.3.

Here the picture is less clear, although if one takes out Luxembourg (the country with the highest GDP per inhabitant in the figure, close to €90,000) then the relation is stronger. In general, the Nordic welfare states spend more on social protection than is spent by countries in central Europe, with Eastern Europe and the UK spending less. The US is also a low spender. In some countries, income benefits are taxable income, whilst in others they are not. This makes comparison difficult.

Therefore, the ability to finance social policy depends not only on the willingness to pay taxes and duties, but also on the size of the economy. A possible reason for this could be that

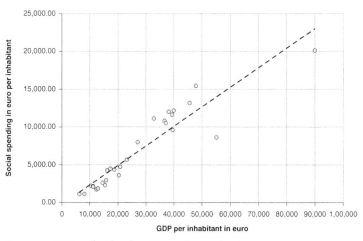

*Figure 4.2*    GDP per head and social spending per head
Source: Based upon Eurostat data, accessed the 31st of May, 2017

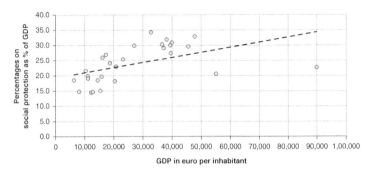

*Figure 4.3*   Spending on social protection as % of GDP and GDP in euro per head in EU countries
Source: Based upon Eurostat data, accessed the 31st of May, 2017

richer countries are able to have a higher level of both public and private consumption. However, the level of spending is also influenced by ideas, historical traditions and national preferences; see also Chapter 5.

The ability to finance welfare also depends on the overall economic development, and therefore it is important to be aware that markets "on their own, are not necessarily efficient, stable, or self-correcting" (Stiglitz, 2014, p. 335); therefore economic policy and corrections of market failure are important issues in order to be able to finance welfare.

## 4.5.  HOW TO CHOOSE THE BEST PATHWAY – EVIDENCE IN SOCIAL POLICY

Social policy has always had to be financed in one way or another, leaving aside the possible impact of preventative initiatives on the long-term level of expenditures (see Debels and Van Hoyweghen, 2018). Given the ability to finance has often been constrained by a lack of either the level of the overall economic development, or the legitimacy of the welfare states and the willingness to pay taxes and duties, there has been an increased need to have informed choices of what works best. Efficiency in administration and delivery of services has seemingly also become more important.

Not all evidence has the same value. There is often argued to be an evidence hierarchy, with systematic reviews and evidence synthesis as the highest level of knowledge. At best, these reviews should be based on randomised control trials as this should make it possible to be sure that it is the social policy intervention that has the impact and not something related to, for example, where people live, their level of education or fluctuations in the business cycle. This can, however, be difficult to achieve in social policy, especially when it relates to services provided by individual persons. This is due to several reasons, one being that the measurement of quality and impact is even more difficult in personal social services, but also that the personal relationship between the cared person and the carer might influence, at least, the experienced quality of a treatment, especially when dealing with treatment for a small number of people (e.g. people with rare types of disability).

Still, evidence-based social policy has been growing in recent years (Greve, 2017; Greener and Greve, 2014). Although, sometimes it might be that policymakers use only the evidence they like – so to speak. For example, if there is an analysis that an intervention is positive and the policymaker likes it, they might argue that they are making the intervention on the basis of evidence; similarly, if they do not like the analysis, they might argue that they have a preference for a different intervention; see also Deeming (2017). However, the movement towards the use of evidence has been in existence for many years, and is based on the tradition of using evidence, especially in relation to health and labour market policy.

There are several issues related to the use of evidence in social policy. One being, as in other sectors, the constant availability of new evidence, which might cause an overload of options, and an awareness that using a new intervention might be too costly as implementation takes time – and also energy from those who will have to implement new initiatives. Furthermore, there might be differences across countries so that what works in one country (or region, municipality) might not necessarily work in another setting. Thus, when doing the evaluation it is also important to describe what has been done, and what theoretical understanding is behind the expectation that an intervention would have a specific outcome. Part of the possible differences in outcome can reflect variations in implementation.

Evaluation is sometimes done on a small-scale project before embarking upon nationwide implementation. This is especially possible when testing new types of services or interventions aimed at different groups in need of specific services. At other times, one can do an *ex post* evaluation of an intervention as a way to look into the long-term effect of an intervention. An example is the analysis of the conditional cash transfers that many countries, especially developing countries, have used as an instrument to get children to attend education as a pre-condition for getting family allowances. The evaluation showed a strong impact on education for children in Brasilia, but also that it was working as a poverty-alleviation instrument (Peruffo and Ferreira, 2017).

However, even if one has the best available evidence, implementation might not always be possible. There can be several reasons for this. One being that the context in which to implement can vary from country to country, and often also within different countries. Those working as professionals might have different types of education, or might have a variety of norms and traditions they would like to implement. In addition, there might not be sufficient financing available as, for example, some medicines can be extremely costly. Still, the aim of using evidence can cause a more efficient use of resources.

## 4.6. SUMMING UP

There has been crisis in welfare states now for many years. There will also be new crises and the main issue is how to reduce the possible negative impact of such crises, and also how to be prepared in order to cope with financial and legitimacy in the different countries. There has at the same time been developments and new areas have been covered. Many countries, for example, have enacted different kinds of leave policies relating to having a child, and also day care for children and long-term care for the elderly have in several countries been developed despite the debate on crisis and retrenchment. Crisis in the wake of the financial crisis has in many countries implied a variety of austerity types of policies with lower level of benefits and weaker welfare services. This has been difficult to finance, and countries have needed to reduce the size of their large public sector deficits.

Social policy needs to be legitimate in the eyes of voters – otherwise they will not vote for candidates and parties – as social policy needs to be financed. At the same time, support to different groups in need in society need not be the same for all persons at all times. Those mainly seen as deserving are those who have all or most of their life participated on the labour market, whereas in several countries migrants and refugees are to a lesser degree seen as deserving, and, thereby there has been a focus on how to make sure that benefits mainly are for natives in a country.

Thus, the development of social policy does not take place in a vacuum, but is dependent on overall societal development, including the ability to finance social policy. It appears that richer countries in general spend more on social policy than less rich countries, albeit the picture is somewhat blurred by differences in preference, ideology and history in the various countries. The ability to finance social policy is also an aspect of the development, as increasing income to the public sector by taxes and duties also imply an option to deliver and pay for more benefits and services. If there is a crisis and public deficit, this might thus not need only to be taken care of by reduction in the level of benefits, but could in principle also be covered by higher levels of taxes and duties. This also helps in explaining why development of social policy is easier in times of economic growth, as there automatically will be higher income for the states, so that it at the same time it is possible to have higher levels of private consumption and public sector consumption.

One way to ensure legitimacy for social policy spending is that the money is spent in such a way that society gets the most value for money, including reducing the risk of criticism for waste of taxpayers' money. This is one reason why evidence-based social policy, despite all the possible difficulties associated with the measurement of evidence, has been increasing in many countries. However, given the possible constraints on social policy, as the demand for service and benefits seems to be able continuously to increase, it is important for users, decision makers and voters that there is as much value for money as possible. This also due to that if money is spent on one project that money can't be spent on another project.

## NOTE

1 See http://ec.europa.eu/eurostat/web/products-eurostat-news/-/DDN-20170705-1?inheritRedirect=true&redirect=%2Feurostat%2F, accessed 7th July 2017.

## REFERENCES

Barr, N. (2012), *Economics of the Welfare State*, 5th edition. Oxford, Oxford University Press.

Blekesaune, M. and Quadagno, J. (2003), Public Attitudes Toward Welfare State Policies: A Comparative Analysis of 24 Nations. *European Sociological Review*, vol. 19, no. 5, pp. 415–427.

Curchin, K. (2017), Using Behavioural Insights to Argue for a Stronger Social Safety Net: Beyond Libertarian Paternalism. *Journal of Social Policy*, vol. 46, no. 2, pp. 231–249.

Debels, A. and Van Hoyweghen, I. (2018), Prevention in Greve, B. ed., *Handbook of the Welfare State*, 2nd edition. Oxon, Routledge.

Deeming, C. (2017), Use and Misuse of Evidence in Greve, B. ed., *Handbook of Social Policy Evaluation*. Cheltenham, Edward Elgar.

Ennser-Jedenastik, L. (2017), Welfare Chauvinism in Populist Radical Right Platforms: The Role of Redistributive Justice Principles. *Social Policy & Administration* http://homepage.univie.ac.at/laurenz.ennser/welfare_chauvinism_WEB.pdf, accepted the 16th of May, 2017.

Farnsworth, K. (2018), Occupational Welfare in Greve, B. ed., *Handbook of the Welfare State*, 2nd edition. Oxon, Routledge.

Greener, I. and Greve, B. ed. (2014), *Evidence and Evaluation in Social Policy*. West Sussex, Wiley Blackwell.

Greve, B. ed. (2017), *Handbook of Social Policy Evaluation*. Cheltenham, Edward Elgar.

Hall, P. (1993), Policy Paradigms, Social Learning, and the State: The Case of Economic Policymaking in Britain. *Comparative Politics*, vol. 25, no. 3, pp. 275–296.

Hinrichs, K. (2018), Pensions in Greve, B. ed., *Handbook of the Welfare State*, 2nd edition. Oxon, Routledge.

Morel, N. and Palme, J. (2018), Financing the Welfare State and the Politics of Taxation in Greve, B. ed., *Handbook of the Welfare State*, 2nd edition. Oxon, Routledge.

OECD. (1981), *Welfare State in Crisis*. Paris, OECD.

Oorschot, W. (2008), Who Should Get What, and Why? in Leibfried, S. and Mau, S. eds., *Welfare States: Construction, Deconstruction, Reconstruction*, pp. 353–368, Cheltenham, Edward Elgar.

Peruffo, M. and Ferreira, P. (2017), The Long-Term Effects of Conditional Cash Transfers on Child Labor and School Enrolment. *Economic Inquiry*, vol. 55, no. 4, pp. 2008–2030. doi: 10.111/ecin.12457.

Roosma, F. Oorschot, W. and Gelissen, J. (2016), The Achilles' Heel of Welfare State Legitimacy: Perceptions of Overuse and Underuse of Social Benefits in Europe. *Journal of European Public Policy*, vol. 23, no. 2, pp. 177–196.

Stiglitz, J. (2014), The Lessons of the North Atlantic Crisis for Economic Theory and Policy in Stiglitz et al. eds., *What Have We Learned? Macroeconomic Policy After the Crisis*. Cambridge, MA, MIT Press.

Taylor-Gooby, P. (2017), Re-Doubling the Crises of the Welfare State: The Impact of Brexit on UK Welfare Politics. *Journal of Social Policy*, 46(4), 815–835. doi:10.1017/S0047279417000538.

Yerkes, M. and Peper, B. (2018), Welfare States and the Life Course in Greve, B. ed., *Handbook of the Welfare State*, 2nd edition. Oxon, Routledge.

# IDEAS AND SOCIAL POLICY

## 5.1. INTRODUCTION

Social policy is not just decided and implemented out of the blue. The field is laden with normative and ideological issues, and this helps to explain why social policy (and labour market policy) is different and varies between countries, and also why it changes over time.

Chapter 5 goes into the reasons why ideas and ideology are important issues in order to understand how and why different systems look like they do, but also the possible reasons for the developments and who the winners and losers are in these changes. The chapter further touches upon the old as well as the new approaches in order to understand social policy, including the Keynesian, neo-liberal and social-investment approaches. These approaches are presented and discussed including differences and similarities, as reflecting upon them can help in explaining the development. Last, the impact of regionalisation (EU) and globalisation are considered. Thus ideas matter – and some of them influence social as well as labour market policy.

## 5.2. WHY IDEAS MATTER

"Ideas can be simply defined as the causal and normative beliefs held by social and policy actors" (Béland and Mahon, 2016, p. 43). Béland has also pointed to how ideas shape actors' perception (Béland, 2018). They also matter because framing suggestions and policies can influence the policy process (Béland, 2005).

This chapter mainly looks into ideas in the field of social policy; however, it is important to be aware that some of the aims and goals (as also touched upon in Chapter 3) have several similarities: "they tend to have different underlying ideas about the causes of unemployment, inequality and poverty" (Peters, 2015, p. 77). Further, having and presenting ideas might also be a way to try to set the agenda for change. Thus, this also points to the fact that being an agenda-setter can have an impact on the possible policy development. However, it can be difficult to set the agenda without having an idea about what is important and why this issue should be part of the discussion. Ideas do not just influence out of the blue, but are part of the process of making decisions, changing legal and economic structures, and trying to get voters to vote for a specific party and/or candidate.

The change in welfare states since the first oil-price crisis (1972/73), and what followed in the industrialised world of stagflation (stagnating economies and high levels of inflation) and increase in unemployment, caused the question to be asked of the effectiveness of the Keynesian demand management to welfare state developments (see more details in Section 5.3). Those in favour of using mainly the market to steer economic and societal development, and with an ambition to have less spent on welfare (especially from the liberal position), gained stronger influence. Thereby, this paved the way in some countries for a reduction in spending and/or a reduction in the level of taxes and duties.

One possible reason was also a dissatisfaction with the fact that welfare states, through their social policy, achieved the ambition of increasing equality and reducing poverty; see Chapter 3. Thus, people on the political left were also disillusioned by welfare states' ability to achieve the expected aims, and therefore were critical of part of the activities, albeit not always for the same reasons as the right. One common criticism relates to the bureaucracy and efficiency of welfare states. Thus, the legitimacy (see also Chapter 4) was in danger, and, as a consequence, possible ideas of how and in what way to change the welfare state were easier to implement.

The development in welfare chauvinism in recent years (see also Chapter 4) and the change in voters' perception of fairness also influence development of ideas, and thereby as to who does and does not get benefits, including the generosity of the various benefits. Thus, policies in other areas (labour market, migration) can have an impact on the ideas and how they might have an impact on decisions.

Ideas in themselves influence voters' perception of what a good social policy is, as do decision makers themselves. This can, for example, be in the form of the impact of public positions and papers from think tanks, etc. Think tanks can, for example, act as pressure groups in favour of expansion of social policy in general or for a specific part of social policy, but can also, as neo-liberal think tanks often do, argue in favour of reduction of social policy as a way to be able to reduce taxes and duties; see also Section 5.3.

Pressure groups can also be employed in certain segment of the welfare state, who argue that if they receive more money then they can deliver better welfare, and can improve well-being in society. In most cases it will be possible to deliver higher level of quality if more money is available; still society will have to prioritise among different aims and options, as there might also be steering problems in ensuring that society gets value for the money. This problem is often labelled the principal–agent problem, where the principal is those who finance an activity, whereas the agent is delivering it. It might be difficult for the principal to know what exactly is delivered by the agent and whether more could be expected for the given sum of money. This explains why a demand for more money is not always accepted, but also why the principal often wants to measure and have information of what is the outcome of spending money within an area.

Naturally, some ideas are first presented or able to influence when there is what has been labelled a window of opportunity (Kingdon, 1984). A window of opportunity can have different forms, but can, for example, be a financial crisis making it more legitimate to reduce the level of benefits than it would be in times of good economic opportunities. In times of crisis, it might thus be more possible to introduce austerity policy in a neo-liberal way (see Section 5.3), whereas in good economic times it can be more difficult to persuade the electorate that this is a necessary policy. The use of language can also influence social policy development (Béland and Petersen, 2014); for example, the use of different connotations of migrants and their access to welfare benefits can influence the discourse and the willingness to pay for benefits if, in this case, migrants have access to these benefits. Making a distinction between them (the others) and us is also a way of influencing perceptions about who should have benefits, under what conditions and how generous the benefits should be.

It has been argued here that ideas matter by setting the agenda; however, they can also influence the choice of policy instrument by learning and diffusion, and this includes evidence-based policy-making (Peters, 2015); see also Greve (2017) and Chapter 4.

## 5.3. KEYNESIAN, NEO-LIBERAL AND SOCIAL INVESTMENT

Other ideas and paradigms could have been used in the presentation; however, the choice has been to have central elements that have influenced welfare state developments, and generally the three paradigms in Table 5.1 have been central and they have also evolved over time.

A paradigm can be understood to be "a framework of ideas and standards that specifies not only the goals of policy and kind of instruments that can be used to attain them, but also the very nature of the problems they are meant to be addressing" (Hall, 1993, p. 279). This choice has further been inspired by Morel, Palier and Palme (2012, Chapter 1), who see social investment as an emerging paradigm, which perhaps will never be a fully-fledged developed paradigm.

Table 5.1 presents the central tenets of the three different paradigms.

It is difficult to know exactly when a paradigm starts and when it ends, and how profound the changes have been, and it is

*Table 5.1*    Central aspects of three paradigms

|  | Keynesian | Neo-liberal | Social investment |
|---|---|---|---|
| **Key values and principles** | Social equality Jobs for all (at that time mainly men) Decommodification | Individual responsibility Any jobs Activation | Social inclusion Quality jobs Capabilities approach Equality of opportunity: prepare rather than repair |
| **Key norms for public action** | Big state Central economic planning Welfare state development | Lean state Deregulation Dismantling of the welfare state | Empowering the state Investment Recasting of the welfare state |
| **Key instruments** | Policies to support demand Development of social insurance schemes for income maintenance Development of the public sector Unemployment compensation | Monetarist economic policies to fight inflation Deregulation of the labour market Privatisation of social and health services, development of capitalisation to finance pension schemes Activation and workfare | Human-capital investment policies to increase competitiveness and job creation Development of social services and policies to support the labour market: early childhood education and care; higher education and life-long training; active labour market policies; policies to support women's employment Flex-security |

Source: Adapted from Morel, Palier and Palme (2012, pp. 12–13, Table 1.1)

also difficult to measure and understand change in ideas (Béland, 2018). Generally, this will only be possible to find out a long time after things have changed. Therefore, the intention here is only to indicate the possible variety of the three different paradigms, also as some might argue that we have not yet seen social investment as an overarching paradigm for social policy development. At the same time, it can be argued that the Keynesian approach has been less strong since the first and second oil-price crisis (see also Chapter 4), whereas the neo-liberal approach has been dominant in many countries since then. However, after the financial crisis in 2008, the ability to let the market steer and manage the development alone has come increasingly into question, and one might even argue that Keynesian types of intervention, and using the instruments as mentioned in Table 5.1, could help many countries in the present economic situation. Besides, it might be that what policymakers name as reforms do not, in reality, change social policy, but are more minor refinements or gradual transformations in the direction of the historical social policy. What follows later is based upon Table 5.1, a short depiction of what and how the three paradigms have as focus with respect to especially social and labour market policy.

The Keynesian paradigms' approach to social policy (and labour market policy) can be argued to have a focus on using the public sector in such a way that the demand would be stable; for example, in times of strong economic activity, the state would dampen it and in times of weak economic activity, the state would support an increase in economic activity. By doing this, the aim of social equality and full employment (or at least a low level of unemployment) could be reached. The state thus has a central role in making the marginal adjustment of the societal economic development. At the same time, the use of the public sector to ensure a high level of employment and some social policy benefits should help in reducing inequality and ensuring at least some guaranteed minimum income. Keynesian welfare states often also have in general higher levels of benefits given, in that they have a double purpose by both ensuring a decent living standard and a stable economic demand in society. Keynesian states will also regulate markets among other things to reduce the negative impact of market failure.

The neo-liberal approach has a strong focus on the market's role, and as already argued a long time ago: "The neo-liberals suggest that the road to growth and prosperity is paved with flexibility and deregulation" (Esping-Andersen, 1996, p. 2). Thus, in this perspective the state should only to a very limited extent provide social policy, and with a strong focus on private provision through use of market elements in the social policy. Taxes and duties should be reduced as much as possible, and deregulation should be done. The expectation of deregulation was that with fewer rules there would be a larger and stronger private sector. Further, with a stronger focus on individual responsibility, and economic growth that would trickle downwards, all in a society would benefit from the development. Increasing inequality was therefore not seen as a problem, as it was the expectation that in the longer run it would also benefit those with lower levels of income. This has been labelled trickle-down economics, as increase in societal wealth was first to the benefit of the rich, but this would later trickle down to the rest of society.

New public management can be argued to be either part of or influenced by the neo-liberal approach by its emphasis on integrating and using a market-type mechanism in the public sector, and also focusing on outsourcing activities to the private sector. Whereas, for the individual user, it might be of less interest whether the provider is public or private, if the service is reliable, of high-quality and low level of user charges, it can have an impact on those working in the service in relation to work and working conditions. For the public sector, the impact of using private providers depends on the area in which this happens and the private companies' function. The overall impact also depends on who finances the activities; if the finance still is mainly public (and the state decides on rules of access and if any then the size of user charge), then the individual using the service might in fact not even be aware of who is providing the service. New public management is not, however, a simple and very precise concept.

The final approach is that of social investment. Social investment has a strong focus on human–capital development, and does not see the public sector as a burden, at least when used effectively, but more as an investment in the future. The focus on capabilities and options has been a central tenet of the social-investment approach, as investment here will improve human capital, and, as a consequence, enable the individual to be able to be self-supporting to a higher degree. Naturally, a key question is what can be understood by investment. This could be "allocation of resources in ways that produce additional, future value-added resources. These additional resources are also known as returns" (Midgley, Dahl and Wright, 2017, p. 14).

Social investment has, for example, been promoted by the European Commission (European Commission, 2013), and can be seen as part of a third way approach (Powell, 2018). The fact that there has been a drive towards social investment can be seen from the many articles on the subject. For some scholars, it has been on the way since the late 1970s as an emergent concept (Kersbergen and Hemerijck, 2012).

Classic, most frequently mentioned examples of what can be argued to be social investment are day care for children and investment into human capital (Hudson and Kühner, 2009). Several other descriptions are also used to show and explain the development in the direction of social investment, such as the new welfare state, new risk welfare, active social welfare, the "third" way (Taylor-Gooby, Gumy and Otto, 2015; Powell, 2018). However, it is also argued that social investment is not new in itself, but a continuation of the "third" way, albeit with a strong aspect of neo-liberal ideas, especially the focus on equality of opportunity instead of equality of outcome. Social investment has also been criticised for forgetting the distributional possible outcome of an active social policy. As with other ideas, this is an open question, and depends on the actual implementation of the policy.

One such criticism of social investment (Nolan, 2013) has been the risk that the focus on social investment (and that public expenditures should be productive) might have a negative impact on social policies' more classical role related to redistribution and reducing the risk of poverty, including also the risk that the focus will be mainly on those who have a long life expectancy ahead of them, and not groups such as the elderly, and thereby the risk of unethical ways of developing social and labour market policy. This cannot, however, be confirmed (Kuitto, 2016). Kuitto also argues that "no uniform shift towards a social investment welfare state can be observed in cross-country comparison at least in terms of governmental spending" (p. 454). In general, it is difficult to measure and estimate the possible impact of social investment.

The fact that ideas influence can, as argued, be that "for example, Keynesian economics provides a means of understanding the business cycle that have beset capitalist economies for centuries" (Peters, 2015, p. 112).

Still, not all countries follow the same pathway and can first be influenced in one direction and then later in another direction. There might even in the future be an amalgamation of the different perspectives. This implies, further, that even if path-dependency is important in order to understand development, changes are frequent and the path is often changed, albeit only gradually.

Historically, countries might also change from one paradigm to another; thus it could be argued that until the oil-price crisis in the 1970s many countries were highly influenced by the Keynesian paradigm. However when that seemingly failed in creating jobs and economic growth, many moved towards a more neo-liberal agenda. Then in the wake of the last financial crisis it has been questioned whether deregulation always is the best remedy for development, and this can be seen as a reason why countries to a certain extent have followed more of a social-investment strategy. That there even can be elements from more than one paradigm in a country's social policy just indicates that the demarcation lines are not always straightforward.

## 5.4.  THE INFLUENCE OF REGIONALISATION AND GLOBALISATION

It is not just only ideas or ideological positions that influence the development of social policy. It has for a long time also been argued that globalisation influences welfare states' development and thereby the options for delivering social policy. There are two central arguments for the possible impact of globalisation on the development in social and also in labour market policy.

One argument is the possibility of financing the welfare state as, with more global interaction, labour and capital can move around more freely. This has implied that the taxes on corporate income have been declining in many countries as one consequence. Many companies are also using legal ways to reduce their tax payment by having companies in tax havens, where taxes are often close to zero. If companies are able to offshore their surplus, then nation states will have less income from taxes, and thereby also less ability to pay for social policy. This can be even more profound in the years to come when production is done through a variety of platforms and/or use of robots.

Another argument is that, with the increased mobility of production, companies have outsourced production to countries with lower costs than the one they are producing in currently. This has reduced the number of traditional jobs, and has (see also Chapters 6 and 7) been part of the reason for unemployment and a pressure on the wage income for low-income earners. If low-income earners are without a job, this increases public sector spending, but also reduces the possible income to the public sector.

The other side of the coin is that globalisation has caused cheaper prices and thereby increased buying power, but also that free trade has improved the option for some companies to earn money, and also ensured higher economic growth.

It might be that globalisation in itself has not reduced the ability to supply and finance social policy, but that it has been used as an argument for cuts that, for some countries with a neo-liberal approach to social policy, have been a central argument for changes they would have preferred anyhow. The central argument has been that without a reduction of the production cost (by lowering taxes and duties), then companies would not be able to compete on the international markets. If there is a need for lower taxes and duties, then this implies less money is available for social and labour market policy.

Regionalisation and its possible impact on social policy varies from region to region around the world. In Europe, there seems to be the most profound impact on social policy from a regional entity compared to other countries around the world. This is in the form of the competences the EU has, and this especially in relation to the free movement of workers and gender equality.

Every citizen in the EU28 countries has the right to move in order to take up a job in another member state. Workers in an EU-member state have the same social rights as workers living in a different member state. EU-member states are not allowed to make rules that can be seen as both a direct and an indirect way to make it difficult to use this right. Therefore, EU-member states cannot give people from other EU-member states lower benefits than its own citizens (on the condition that they fulfil the country's regulation with regard to the specific benefit); see further the elaboration in Section 6.6. This has raised discussions, for example, on whether family allowances shall be the same for all, as children in families receiving family allowances might not necessarily live in the country where the person is working.

The principle of gender-equal treatment, which was part of the original Treaty of Rome in 1957, has, as an example, the implication that the retirement age shall be the same for men and women, and that in principle there shall be equal wages for men and women when doing the same job. Therefore, this influences development. However, there are still unequal levels of wages for men and women, reflecting that a principle might not always be possible to implement in practice. In this case also due to that the demand for equality is a demand for the same wage for the same job, defining and understanding what the same job is might not always be an easy task.

There are also directives which are directly applicable in EU-member states regarding leave, working time, and safety and security in the workplace. These have been implemented with the purpose of reducing the risk that a low level of, for example, safety at the workplace could be an issue for competition.

So, albeit social policy in principle in the EU is national, there are implications hereof.

## 5.5. SUMMING UP

Ideas do not just float in midair. They have an impact on social policy and its development around the globe, an impact which is stronger in some countries than in others, and stronger at some times than others. For example, in times of economic crisis, changes might be pushed through more easily as they are argued to be "necessary". This was the case after the oil-price crisis in the 1970s and after the financial crisis starting in 2008. The impact of ideas might be difficult to measure; however, it seems that there are several paradigms, and that which one is more important has changed over time and will presumably continue to differ over time, and countries influenced by one paradigm might change as a consequence of the impact of ideas.

Keynesian, neo-liberal and social investment are some of the ideas that have briefly been presented, as they seem to be the ones that have had the strongest impact on the understanding of the aim and purposes of social and labour market policy, and further how they in the best way, according to the ideas behind the paradigm, can develop. Each has a different focus on the role of the state, the market and civil society, and each has different perceptions about what the impact will be of using a variety of instruments, with the social-investment perspective as the least developed in that regard, and with a more varied understanding of the consequence of social spending on societies' development.

The growing internationalisation and the consequence on nation states of globalisation indicate even more that social policy is not formed in a vacuum, but highly influenced by what happens in other countries. As a consequence national economies are highly influenced by international development, and thereby their ability to finance social policies.

So, even if we see path-dependency, we are also witnessing gradual and sometimes strong change in the policies – and therefore the variation and interpretation of social policy also change over time. We see further developments in the overall level of spending and structure of social policy reflecting changes in ideas, but also changes in economic options.

## REFERENCES

Béland, D. (2005), Ideas and Social Policy: An Institutionalist Perspective. *Social Policy & Administration*, vol. 39, no. 1, pp. 1–18.

Béland, D. (2018), How Ideas Impact Social Policy, in Greve, B. ed., *The Routledge Handbook of the Welfare State*, 2nd edition. Oxon, Routledge.

Béland, D. and Mahon, R. (2016), *Advanced Introduction to Social Policy*. Cheltenham, Edward Elgar.

Béland, D. and Petersen, K. (2014), *Analysing Social Policy Concepts and Language*. Bristol, Policy Press.

Esping-Andersen, G. ed. (1996), *Welfare States in Transition: National Adaptations in Global Economies*. London, Sage.

European Commission (2013), *Social Investment Package*. Brussels, EU.

Greve, B. ed. (2017), *Handbook of Social Policy Evaluation*. Cheltenham, Edward Elgar.

Hall, P. (1993), Policy Paradigms, Social Learning and the State: The Case of Economic Policy-Making in Britain. *Comparative Politics*, vol. 25, no. 3, pp. 275–296.

Hudson, J. and Kühner, S. (2009), Towards Productive Welfare? A Comparative Analysis of 23 OECD Countries. *Journal of European Social Policy*, vol. 19, no. 1, pp. 34–46.

Kersbergen, K. and Hemerijck, A. (2012), Two Decades of Change in Europe: The Emergence of the Social Investment State. *Journal of Social Policy*, vol. 41, no. 3, pp. 475–492.

Kingdon, J. (1984), *Agendas, Alternatives and Public Policies*. Boston, MA, Little Brown Book.

Kuitto, K. (2016), From Social Security to Social Investment? Compensating and Social Investment Welfare Policies in a Life-Course Perspective. *Journal of European Social Policy*, vol. 26, no. 5, pp. 442–459.

Midgley, J., Dahl, E. and Wright, A. ed. (2017), *Social Investment and Social Welfare: International and Critical Perspectives*. Cheltenham, Edward Elgar.

Morel, N., Palier, B. and Palme, J. (2012), *Towards a Social Investment Welfare State?* Bristol, Policy Press.

Nolan, B. (2013), What Use Is 'Social Investment'? *Journal of European Social Policy*, vol. 23, no. 5, pp. 459–468.

Peters, B. G. (2015), *Advanced Introduction to Public Policy*, Cheltenham, Edward Elgar.

Powell, M. (2018), The Third Way in Greve, B. ed., *The Routledge Handbook of the Welfare State*, 2nd edition. Oxon, Routledge.

Taylor-Gooby, P. (2017), Re-Doubling the Crises of the Welfare State: The Impact of Brexit on UK Welfare Politics. *Journal of Social Policy*, pp. 1–21 doi: 10.1017/S0047279417000538.

Taylor-Gooby, P., Gumy, J. and Otto, A. (2015), Can 'New Welfare' Address Poverty through More and Better Jobs? *Journal of Social Policy*, vol. 44, no. 1, 83–104. doi:10.1017/S0047279414000403.

# LABOUR MARKET POLICY

## 6.1. INTRODUCTION

Having a job with a good and stable income is often a central aspect of having a good life, thus as with social policy (see Chapter 3), labour market policy is a very important and central issue. This is because a job gives access to income, but also social contact and esteem if one is in the working age group.

The preceding chapters have focused on social policy. Making a distinction between social and labour market policy is, perhaps, superficial, as the access to several benefits in many countries depends on being in, or having had, a job. Nevertheless, the difference is that labour market policy clearly revolves around how to understand the functioning of the labour market. Thus, the first issue is to discuss more precisely what a labour market is – or perhaps at the outset to be aware that there are many and very varied types of labour market. In Section 6.2, the focus is on what a labour market is, and how to explain the level of employment and unemployment, and the possible reasons for this.

The reasons for unemployment need not be the same over time and the same in all countries. Besides the explanations that are given in Section 6.2, Section 6.3 focuses on what has been labelled the fourth industrial revolution and its possible impact on the labour market. Thus, the section also presents the debate on the future of work (Greve, 2017b). This is combined with how modern technology might influence the understanding of the labour market. There are a variety of concepts that can be used to understand the impact of these changes, also concepts that have been used to explain the historical development. These include concepts such as dualisation, insider/outsider and the precariat, which are central to the discussion in Section 6.4.

Ways of combining flexibility and security (flexicurity) have become high on the agenda both at the supranational and national levels. Section 6.5 discusses how to understand the concept and its different connotations in different welfare states, including links to a discussion on social security benefits (unemployment and social assistance), for example what is often also labelled passive labour market policy. The free movement of workers, especially with a focus on the EU, which has had an impact on the labour market, and is also questioned in some countries, is the focus in Section 6.6. The subject of the alternatives to a flexible labour market, for example the ALMP, is returned to in Chapter 7. Lastly, the chapter is summed up.

## 6.2. WHAT IS A LABOUR MARKET AND EMPLOYMENT/UNEMPLOYMENT?

Overall, in principle the labour market is the market for buying and selling labour. This is what is labelled as the commodification of labour. Buying and selling implies that a worker is willing to work and accept the wage and working conditions for a specific job, and that an employer is willing to employ a person for a specific kind of job. Understood in this sense, the labour market is, in many ways, like many other markets for different kinds of commodities.

Wages are the prices on the labour market and, in many countries, collective agreements influence the level of wages and working conditions. Many countries also have a legally decided minimum income.

A central difference between the labour market and other markets is naturally that a person can accept or decline a job, except implicitly if this has consequences for receiving social security benefits, whereas this is not the case for goods on other markets. Still, the similarity is that a person who wants to sell his/her labour needs to find a buyer, and they must agree upon wages and working conditions. These might be dependent on a collective wage agreement with only limited options for individual negotiation of the wage level, but can also be fully individually agreed. There are also some EU rules and national rules which have to be fulfilled, such as working time, safety at the workplace and minimum income in some countries.

Still, this does not give a full explanation of what a labour market is. This is because there is not just one labour market. Labour markets are or might be locally, regionally, nationally and globally different; they can be different in big cities compared to the countryside; they can be different depending on the structure of the specific economy, for example, the degree of industrialisation and service approach in the economy; they can also be different depending on the qualifications of the workers available in an area or the production possible in a specific geographical area.

Already from these different ways of understanding the labour market, it is obvious that there might also be different types of unemployment and various reasons for the unemployment.

Looking at the supply side, an argument is that if the supplier of labour is not willing to accept the given wage in an area or for a specific type of job, then the person is voluntarily unemployed. Supply-side economists argue that the level of employment in the long run depends on the total labour supply.

The size of the labour supply and the demand for labour have, thereby, two other central issues.

Demand to a large degree depends on the overall economic activity in a society, so that, for example, in the wake of the last financial crisis the number of jobs fell strongly in many sectors and the unemployment rate increased. However, the demand might change between different types of jobs, due to, for example, technological development (see Section 6.3). It might also depend on the expectation of the future development, so that companies expecting an increase in the demand for their goods and services will hire people, or retain otherwise surplus employees, whom they expect to be able to use shortly. Governments might, by an expansive (contractive) economic policy, ensure higher (lower) demand for labour. Overall, demand is also influenced by the development in productivity.

The supply of labour is dependent on many different issues. It depends on age, push or drive factors related to migration, level of benefits, situation of a spouse/relative, geographical position, etc. It can also depend on the ability to get a job and the wage level.

Over the life course, people's participation on the labour market related to age follows a curve, first increasing (typically after education) and then decreasing when retiring on reaching the pension age. There is variation of the age of entering and leaving the labour market in different countries. Entering the labour market depends on how long is spent in education, and also, in several countries, for women whether or not they have a child. Some leave the labour market earlier than others, for example, due to a work accident, needing to take care of a dependent relative, or losing their job after the closure of a company and experiencing (due to age, lack of upskilling, etc.) difficulties in re-entering the labour market. People with different degrees of disabilities often have a lower level of attachment to the labour markets than others.

Migration and the participation on the labour market can also vary. Those migrating because there are pull-factors (e.g. someone demanding their work) will have good options to have a job and be on the labour market, whereas those who, for one reason or another, have been pushed to migrate might have more difficulties in getting a job. This can be due to the lack of language abilities, lack of recognition of formal as well as informal qualifications, but also discrimination against people coming from other countries (Brochman and Dølvik, 2018). Overall, migrants often have a weaker position on the labour market than native persons.

Employment prospects are better in some areas than in others, thus people's ability to get a job can vary, in addition to the issue of whether people, in fact, try to get a job.

The level of social benefits is also argued to influence whether people are in jobs, as it is argued that there should be economic incentives to search for a job. There is no knowledge about how strong this incentive needs to be as non-monetary factors also influence people's well-being (see Chapter 3), and losing a job has a negative impact on the individual's level of happiness (Chung, 2016). The level of benefits needs to be looked upon in connection with the wage level, so that if the wage level is very low this might also influence the labour supply. The reason for a change in well-being relates to different issues, a central aspect of which is that the loss of a job brings with it a loss of social contact, and also the connected loss of status and the means to use one's abilities (Sage, 2017).

Last, health and the ability to work will influence the ability to supply work and also whether one is able to get a job, as those who have many days absent from work due to sickness also have a higher risk of being sacked in times of recession.

Figure 6.1 shows a snapshot of the situation on the EU labour market in 2016 – showing the number of people in jobs, unemployed and underemployed.

Figure 6.1 is an indication of both the size of the situation and the fact that there is a labour supply available, but not at present on the labour market. It also shows that there are 45 million working part time. In all countries, there are more women working part time than men, and part-time work can be voluntary – as a way of combining work and family life – but can also be involuntary, implying that the family has lower income than they would prefer. Naturally, here as in other parts of the labour markets there will be variations also across countries – in some countries more people are underemployed, more people are working part time, but still the figure is a clear indication of labour resources available around in Europe if there is a demand for the labour.

The employment rate differs among countries, as shown in Figure 6.2.

Figure 6.2 shows the variation in the employment rate across Europe – being highest in the Northern and Western parts of Europe, and lowest in Southern Europe. Eastern European countries have both high and low levels, so the picture does not follow the classical way of welfare regimes (Greve, 2018). This is due to differences in historical legacy, but also differences with

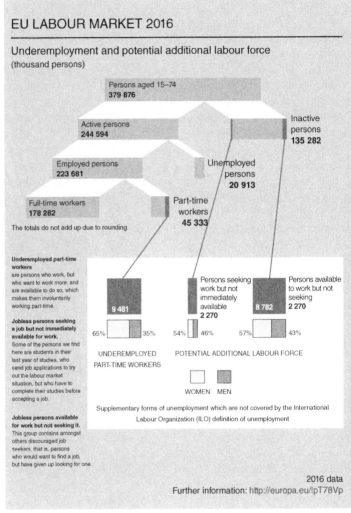

*Figure 6.1*   EU labour market 2016

regard to when women entered the labour market – which first
happened in the Nordic and Eastern European countries. So
if in all countries women gradually take up jobs on the labour
market then, over time, the variation in employment rates will

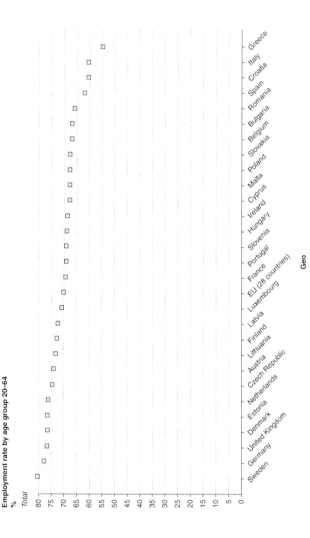

Figure 6.2    Employment rate by age (20–64) in EU-member states in 2015

also be smaller across countries. Equality of men and women related to participation on the labour market can have different reasons, one being (see also Chapter 2) the difference in the level of affordable child care services. Historical norms of the division between state and civil society, and the tradition of a male-breadwinner system, also have an impact. In recent years, in most countries, there has been a catching up, so that the participation rate of men and women now is closer to each other than previously. However, in many countries we still see gender-segregated labour markets, where men to a larger degree work in the private sector, and women in the public or service sectors. This is also depicted in Table 6.1, which shows the employment rate for the 15–64 age group, the young and the older workers in the EU-member states in 2015.

Table 6.1 shows several elements at the same time. One is that the young, mainly due to being in education, have a lower level of attachment to the labour market. Another is the closing gap between men's and women's labour force participation, where the gap was 14.3 percentage points in 2006 and was reduced to 10.5 points in 2015. A third is that people aged 55–64 seem to stay longer on the labour market than previously – witnessed by the increasing labour force participation rate for both men and women, albeit also showing a lower level of participation

*Table 6.1* Employment rate in EU28 for men and women in different age groups

| EU28 | 2006 | 2009 | 2012 | 2015 |
|---|---|---|---|---|
| 15–24 all | 36.4 | 34.8 | 32.5 | 33.1 |
| 15–24 male | 39.3 | 36.8 | 34.4 | 34.9 |
| 15–24 female | 33.4 | 32.8 | 30.5 | 31.3 |
| 15–64 all | 64.3 | 64.5 | 64.1 | 65.6 |
| 15–64 male | 71.5 | 70.6 | 69.6 | 70.9 |
| 15–64 female | 57.2 | 58.4 | 58.6 | 60.4 |
| 55–64 all | 43.3 | 45.9 | 48.7 | 53.3 |
| 55–64 male | 52.5 | 54.6 | 56.2 | 60.2 |
| 55–64 female | 34.7 | 37.7 | 41.7 | 46.9 |

Source: http://ec.europa.eu/eurostat/tgm/table.do?tab=table&plugin=1&language=en&pcode=t2020_10, accessed the 17th of April 2017

rate than the 15–64 age group. The table only to a more limited extent shows the impact of the financial crisis on the labour force situation for men and women. This is shown in Figure 6.3, which sets out the unemployment rate for men and women.

Figure 6.3 reveals two elements for all 28 EU countries. The first is the profound impact of the financial crisis on the level of the unemployment rate, which increased from around 7% to close to 11% at its highest level. The second is that the unemployment rate for men and women on the labour market is now almost equal, whereas in 2007–09 it was higher for women than for men. Thus, the figure reveals one of the core reasons for the level of unemployment: fluctuations in the economy. Albeit some countries were harder hit than others. Besides that we have witnessed that especially young people were hard hit by the financial crisis and were having difficulty entering the labour market – even when having taken an education. Still, for those between 15–24 years of age in Europe the unemployment rate is close to 20%, around 10% for those between 25–29 years of age and around 6% for other age groups.

Reasons for unemployment other than business fluctuations are seasonal differences in the level of unemployment – in most countries, unemployment is lowest during the summertime, as

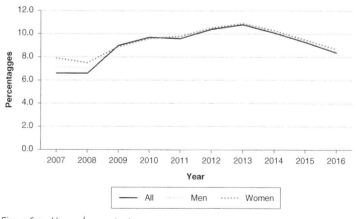

*Figure 6.3*   Unemployment rate 2007–2015
Source: Eurostat, accessed the 17th of April 2017

there is much more work, for example, in agriculture, construction and tourism. Unemployment can also be due to regional differences as the availability of jobs differs – often more and different types of jobs are available in cities than in the countryside.

Another reason for becoming unemployed can be due to structural and technological developments. Structural differences refer to change in societal structure – such as, historically, fewer jobs in agriculture, followed by fewer jobs in industry, and now there might also be a trend of fewer jobs in the services sector. This is due to new technologies, which is the focus of Section 6.3.

Not all who want a job can get one – and there might be various types of discrimination on the labour market. This is despite the fact that, in most countries, discrimination on the grounds of gender, ethnicity, disability and religion is not allowed. However, discrimination can take place indirectly as employers argue that they have chosen another person who they deemed better able to do the job. Discrimination against different groups can also relate to prejudice by employers, for example, they may be scared to employ a person within a specific group without looking into the individual person's qualifications. Further, they might expect unemployed people, especially the long-term unemployed, to have a lower level of productivity. In relation to young women, as an example, the fear of a long maternity leave can have the implication that some companies will not employ them.

In all countries, people with disabilities have a lower attachment to the labour market than other people. This can reflect discrimination, but also that some people with disabilities have less education than others.

For migrants, there is the risk that their qualifications are not recognised, they do not know the language in the country they are now working in, and/or the working culture, combined with cultural issues in the family. Thus, in most countries, migrants (except those with a high level of qualifications) often have a lower level of attainment to the labour market. In Europe, people from outside Europe also often have a lower participation rate.

The attachment to the labour market is also influenced by the level of education, so that people with higher levels of education often have better options. Furthermore, the unemployment rate is also higher, in general, for unskilled than for skilled labour, and the higher the educational attainment level is the lower the unemployment rate is. This can naturally vary between different kinds of professions and over time, but as a general rule this is the picture on most countries' labour markets.

So, there are many and varied reasons for the difference in the employment and unemployment rates. However, before embarking upon an analysis of these issues and the impact of technology, having a job does not necessarily imply that people have the job they want, or the number of hours they want to work. Therefore, there is also the concept of underemployment. This can have different dimensions:

> Hours – e.g. fewer hours so that a person involuntarily works less than full time
>
> Income – e.g. not providing income above the poverty line even if working full time
>
> Skill – e.g. a person is not able to use their skills and training
>
> Status – e.g. the job is providing less status than expected based upon background
>
> (Friedland and Price, 2003)

Underemployment has been on the increase in recent years, albeit the measurable indicator looks especially at the number of hours of the type of underemployment, whereas it is much more difficult to measure the other dimensions related to underemployment, for example, skills and income.

Those presumably most hit by underemployment are those who have a less stable attachment to the labour market (see also Section 6.4), and they might even prefer to take an unsure temporary job in order to be on the labour market (Pearson, 2015).

A person not able to use his/her skills can be argued to be overqualified for the job, and when this is the case there is a risk that persons with lower levels of qualifications are less able to get a job, as they are pushed out of their job by people with higher levels of qualifications.

An issue related to insider/outsider, precariousness and dualisation on the labour market (see Section 6.4) is thus the type of job people have. Jobs can be permanent or temporary. A temporary job is, as the name indicates, not a permanent position, and the individual will be unemployed if the contract is not renewed or the individual can get another job. Having a temporary job can be voluntary, as is often the case especially for young people; however, the job might not be voluntary and might leave the person in an unsecure situation. Temporary jobs can be important for companies, as they give them flexibility. Jobs can also be full time and part time, and in most countries more women than men work part time – this can be both voluntary as a way to combine work and family life, but can also reflect that a person who wants to work more is not able to get a sufficient number of hours, for example underemployment.

There are thus many and varied types of jobs, and the fourth industrial revolution (as described in more detail in Section 6.3) is a further challenge for the developments on the labour markets. The many and new forms of employment which are not standard are depicted in Table 6.2. According to the OECD definition, non-standard jobs include: self-employment (own account workers), temporary or fixed-term contracts, and part-time work. The ILO defines non-standard jobs as

> jobs that fall outside the realm of standard work arrangement, including temporary or fixed-term contracts, temporary agency or dispatched work, dependent self-employment, as well as part-time work, including marginal part-time work, which is characterised by short, variable, and often unpredictable hours.
>
> (Spasova, Bouget, Ghailani and Vanhercke, 2017, p. 20)

Whether or not part-time jobs are non-standard can be discussed as for some, this is a voluntary choice in order to better be able to ensure a good work–family life balance, whilst for others it can be forced upon them and cause a situation of working poor.

Besides this there has also been a development of increasing numbers of self-employed people, sometimes described as bogus self-employment, meaning that they are not employed and work more or less only for one company on a "self-employed" basis thereby they do not need to be paid the wage in the collective agreement and/or the state minimum wage.

*Table 6.2*   New forms of employment

| New forms of employment (NFE) | Characteristics |
| --- | --- |
| Employee sharing | An individual worker is jointly hired by a group of employers to meet the human resources needs of various companies. |
| Job sharing | An employer hires two or more workers to jointly fill a specific job, combining two or more part-time jobs into a full-time position. |
| Interim management | Highly skilled experts are hired temporarily for a specific project or to solve a specific problem. |
| Casual work | An employer is not obliged to provide work regularly to the employees, but has the flexibility of calling them in on demand. |
| ICT-based mobile work | Workers can do their job from any place at any time, supported by modern technologies. |
| Voucher-based work | The employment relationship is based on payment for services with a voucher purchased from an authorised organisation that covers both pay and social security contributions. |
| Portfolio work | A self-employed individual works for a large number of clients, doing small-scale jobs for each of them. |
| Crowd employment | An online platform matches employers and workers, often with a larger task being split up and divided among a virtual cloud of workers. |
| Collaborative employment | Freelancers, the self-employed or micro-enterprises cooperate in some way to overcome limitations of size and professional isolation. |

Source: Spasova, Bouget, Ghailani and Vanhercke (2017, p. 27)

Furthermore, many of those working in these new forms of jobs and self-employment are often, depending on which country they live in, less covered by social policy. They are covered by the more universal types of schemes (such as access to hospitals, care for children and elderly), but often less by different types of income transfers. They will typically be covered by basic state pension, but often not with unemployment benefit, social assistance and sickness benefit. Thus, these new types of jobs where the number of hours can be unsure also cause the risk of social insecurity.

A high degree of insecurity of job, income and social benefits is also experienced by the number of workers, especially in the care sector, who work through cash-for-care schemes or even as illegal migrants. They have been part of a response to the need for care, especially for the elderly, but are often in a precarious situation (Morel, 2015); see also Section 6.4.

## 6.3. FOURTH INDUSTRIAL REVOLUTION

Technological development has always had an impact on which jobs are available, and what types of jobs are no longer in demand (Greve, 2017a; Greve, 2017b). Whenever new inventions have come about, people with specific skills have had to look for other types of jobs. New jobs have also been created, and thus provide new options for many people. The historical development from agrarian societies to industrialisation and then towards service economies has had a profound impact on the qualifications requested at the labour market.

The implication of the increasing interconnectedness and globalisation is that goods and services can be produced anywhere in the globe and then transported to the place where they will be used. Thereby implying that national production has gradually become more specialised, and therefore that national labour markets have also become gradually more specialised.

The question now is whether we are on the brink of a completely new development where the demand for humans as a labour force is entering a new phase. This could be with a reduced demand for labour due to the use of new technology (including robots), implying that it will be difficult to continue along the historical path with a high level of employment for everyone in society, and/or whether the development will increase inequality among people so that far more people will be outside or only to a limited extent on the labour market, implying a lower income for these people than for those in stable jobs.

One way of making a distinction between different types of jobs could be, as shown in Table 6.3, the difference between routine and non-routine jobs.

Thus, the argument is that especially jobs with many routine elements could be automated. However, even in non-routine jobs, there are elements that, today, by splitting tasks into smaller units, might be changed and job numbers reduced with the use

*Table 6.3*  Skills, risk and consequences of automation split between routine and non-routine work

|  | Routine | Non-routine |
|---|---|---|
| Analytical and interactive tasks | Substantial substitution | Strong complementarities |
| Manual tasks | Substantial substitution | Limited opportunities for substitution or complementarity |

Source: Based on Autor, Levy and Murnane (2003, p. 1286)

of information technology (IT). To give a few examples, jobs such as legal writing and medical diagnosis might be split so that part of the jobs can be taken over by the use of IT. Thus, with such a change, a stronger division between insiders and outsiders seems to be a logical consequence in the future. There are some types of jobs that are constantly changed, so that what used to be assembly work is no longer able to be routinized much more as technology has already replaced many jobs. Due to the change in the number of jobs in the industrial sector, which has already happened in several countries (see Pfeiffer, 2016), many people with skills related to this kind of production will have difficulties in getting another job. However, even if there is a need for controlling the work of robots, they will presumably be more able in the future to be self-diagnostic, and thus production might be done nearly without the involvement of humans.

Thus, a reason for the impact of new technologies is that many more functions might be done by robots than previously, and many more functions transferred from humans to machines (Kaplan, 2015). Jobs where there is some kind of routine, as indicated in Table 6.2, can more easily be replaced than more complicated jobs and jobs where there is a need for personal interaction, as in many welfare sectors.

The counterargument is that, historically, technology has wiped jobs away, but new jobs and new positions have emerged, so what we are witnessing is just a continuation of a historical constant change of types of jobs. Still, the transformation we are witnessing today seems to be changing the labour market to a stronger extent and more dramatically, and thus having a profound influence on welfare states (Greve, 2017b).

While the use of new technologies might sweep a large number of jobs away, it will also have a beneficial impact on the working conditions in several areas. For example, the risk of having to lift heavy things might be reduced and thereby physical injuries might be reduced.

One of the possible consequences of new technologies and the use of platforms to produce services is an increase in people working as so-called self-employed (i.e. they are not employed). These people will be less covered by social security, and might also have lower wages as they are not covered by collective agreements of minimum wages.

Overall, this points to the fact that technological developments have both a positive and negative impact on the labour market. They might improve working conditions and reduce the risk that workers will have to leave the labour market as early as previously. At the same time, there is a strong risk that many workers will be obsolete and that their competences will no longer be in demand, so that more people will be unemployed for longer time periods during their working life, and some might have difficulties in entering the labour market at all.

## 6.4. CENTRAL CONCEPTS TO UNDERSTAND THE DEVELOPMENT

In this section, the central concepts that have been used to explain and inform on the development on the labour market are presented. They have in common that they try to depict variations, and to a certain extent also the possible outcomes of the differences in being or not being on the labour market, and the possibility of being able to enter or not enter the labour market. The concepts that are presented include dualisation, segmentation, job-polarisation, insider/outsider and the precariat. They overlap, but they are also concepts that should help in the understanding of why some have jobs, some have good jobs, some have high wages, whereas others only to a more limited extent have a job, which is in fact often outside the labour market, and if they do have a job it is poorly paid and with lack of good working conditions. These concepts need to be seen in relation to the different types of jobs as described in Section 6.2

(such as temporary, underemployment, overqualification, self-employment [especially bogus] and other non-standard jobs).

Dualisation can have different forms. The possible three different forms can be understood by focusing on: deepening, widening and new institutional dualism (Emmenegger et al., 2012). Segmentation on the labour market refers to, as the word indicates, the fact that there are different segments on the labour market. They can vary in demand for qualification, job security, level of wages, etc. Emmenegger et al. argue that the difference between the concepts of dualisation and segmentation includes the fact that polarisation does not necessarily focus on the politics of change. This in contrast to dualisation, which "implies that policies increasingly differentiate rights, entitlements, and services provided to different categories of recipients" (Emmenegger et al., 2012, p. 10). Dualisation can further vary over time and have a different impact depending on the social policy pursued in a country.

Job-polarisation, compared to the insider/outsider theory (see later), refers to the fact that there will be expansion of the highest and lowest paid jobs compared to the middle-wage jobs, implying task-based technological change – which historically, especially, has had a negative impact on the unskilled – will also have an impact on middle-wage jobs. A possible new development might further be that technology also has a stronger impact on high-skilled jobs because (as argued in Section 6.3) if they can be split into smaller parts more easily than previously, they can be taken over by robots. Offshoring jobs with low technology also implies a risk of polarisation (OECD, 2016). Polarisation can be measured by considering the change in occupations with high, middle and low income. Overall in Europe (data are for 16 western countries between 1993 and 2010), the changes have been:

| | |
|---|---|
| High-paying occupations | +5.62 |
| Middling occupations | −9.27 |
| Low-paying occupations | +3.65 |

(Goos, Manning and Salomons, 2014, p. 2512)

Overall, the picture was the same in all 16 countries, with only some limited variation. Polarisation is thus a tendency already witnessed in relation to a long-term decline in the middle-skill types of jobs (Rutledge and Guan, 2015); however, with the possibility that moving into the fourth industrial revolution will influence to a greater extent, or will influence a greater number of, low-paying occupations and some of the high-paying occupations.

There are especially two types of understanding of the economic growth used to explain the development towards polarisation. If it is skill-biased technological change, this will be less of a problem, whereas routine-based technological change will have a stronger negative impact on the labour market. The polarisation as shown previously is that overall there is some "evidence of polarisation, a trend that becomes more obvious during recessions" (Eurofound, 2016, p. 11). However, Eurofound argues that since 1998 there have been tendencies towards upgrading.

A possible growing divide on the labour market will imply a strong risk that societies will become more divided. This is due to differences in access in many welfare states to different types of benefits related to having a job, but naturally also as high-income groups are able to buy more goods and services than low-income households. This is also the case as "outsiders are defined as the (working) poor that would have to rely on modest (largely means-tested) public provision, primarily intended to ameliorate poverty" (Seeleib-Kaiser, 2013, p. 62). Thus, being an outsider not only influences access to jobs, but also to welfare and social policy benefits. Or to put it another way, a "differentiating between social protection insiders and outsiders" (Seeleib-Kaiser, 2016, p. 222).

Differences between outsiders' and insiders' attachment to the labour market and possible consequences hereof has long been discussed, starting with Doeringer and Piore (1971), and later Lindbeck and Snower (1986), who instead used the terms "core" and "periphery" of workers. Insiders get the good, stable jobs with high income, whereas the outsiders have unstable jobs often at lower wage levels.

As with the other concepts, one argument is that the position at the labour market reflects the productivity of the workers, as those in the core are expected to be more productive than those on the periphery. In contrast hereto, it is argued with a focus on powers that the segmentation and dualisation on the labour market are a consequence of power-resources of the actors on the labour market; see also Chapter 2 on central actors. In the varieties of capitalism approaches to understand welfare state development, there has also been a focus on possible consequences due to the changes. A central argument highlighting the relationship of labour markets to national institutional structures is:

> Whether organised labour and capital use labour shedding to ease the costs of economic adjustment while maintaining industrial peace depends not only on the available pathways to public pre-retirement programmes but also on the exigencies of national labour relations and production systems at the workplace.
>
> (Ebbinghaus and Manow, 2001, p. 14)

The concept of the precariat refers to those working in precarious jobs, a concept especially Standing has pointed to (Standing, 2014). He has argued that people who lack seven forms of labour-related security – labour market security, employment security, job security, work security, skill reproduction security, income security, representation security (Standing, 2011, p. 10) – will be working in the precariat, albeit it is not clear whether and how many of those types one need to fulfil in order to be in the precariat. It is therefore also difficult to measure the size of the precariat. However, it points to a growing divide on the labour market, and that many, including many self-employed, will be in positions where their economic and social security is at a very low level. The security forms that Standing has pointed to in many ways also reflect concepts from the literature on flexicurity, another central issue (presented in Section 6.5).

One consequence of the situation continuing is that becoming unemployed can have a scarring effect. This can be on the individual's trust in what he/she is able to achieve, as long periods of unemployment can undermine people's confidence and thereby reduce the level of human capital, but also that it might deter an employer to take on an unemployed person as the unemployed are seen as having fewer competences than those who are employed. Therefore, longer periods of unemployment can have stronger detrimental effects than short periods – and for a newly educated person it is first after a time of unemployment that this can be an issue.

## 6.5. FLEXICURITY – AS BUZZWORD

Flexicurity understood simply is how to combine security for workers with flexibility for employers (for an overview, see Tros and Wilthagen, 2013). It has also been endorsed by the EU as important. Table 6.4 shows the possible trade-offs between the concept.

Without going into much detail, Table 6.4 reflects the fact that there are a number of different types of security and flexibility, which can overlap and interact in a number of ways. Job security refers to staying in the same job, whereas employment security relates to having a job (and this can be achieved by both the overall economic policy and ALMP; see Chapter 7). Income security is related to the person's economic situation in case of unemployment, and here the social policy system (see Chapter 3) is the important element as a more generous income benefit system implies a higher degree of economic security. Flexibility refers to how and whether it is possible to shift the number of people in a company, the functions they do and the level of wages and other types of payment. These can also be combined in large numbers.

The generosity of the passive labour market policy (unemployment benefits and early retirement benefits) can have an impact on the degree of economic security in case of losing one's job. This generosity varies a lot between countries. The

*Table 6.4*   Trade-offs and interconnections between types of flexibility and types of security

|  | Job security | Employment security | Income security | Combination security |
|---|---|---|---|---|
| Flexibility: external-numerical internal-numerical |  |  |  |  |
| Functional |  |  |  |  |
| Wages/variable pay |  |  |  |  |

Source: Tros and Wilthagen (2013, p. 128)

tendencies in the last 15–20 years have, in many countries, been to reduce economic security in case of unemployment. Two types of arguments have been related to this, One being a lack of financial means to pay out benefits. The other being that there shall be a high economic incentive to take up a job – or, as sometimes argued, any job – and if the benefit is high it is argued that some will prefer the benefit instead of a job. However, this argument rests upon the fact that money is the only reason to have and be willing to work in a job. For some, in order to have a high level of well-being it is a very important aspect to have job, as this influences self-realisation, opens the way for social contacts, etc. Thus, whether or not lower economic benefits increase the incentives to take up a job is an open question. This is because the availability of jobs also depends on the economic situation in the country, so that in times of strong economic activity there are more jobs than in times of low economic activity. Having to take any job also increases the risk of working poor, for example, even if having a job the income might be below the poverty line. Early retirement benefit has the possible impact that people no longer able to work can leave the labour market. This benefit is different in many countries, and has been reduced as there has been an interest in getting people to stay longer on the labour market due to demographic ageing.

Flexibility in and across companies is also influenced by the abilities of people to continue their education and constantly be upgraded – and thus the idea of life-long learning will have an impact on the options and possibilities for persons to be flexible over time.

The many and varied interpretations of, and elements included in, flexicurity can be a reason for the fact that so many countries argue that they have a flexicurity approach on the labour market, as the theory does not have any specific criteria for what should be fulfilled in order to label a system flexicurity.

There are here, as in many other spheres of societies, different interests at stake.

Employers will often prefer as large a flexibility as possible, as this will make it easier for them to reduce the overall level of costs. Their position on the level of benefit can partly depend on who is going to finance the benefit, but also upon their view about the possible impact of generous benefits on the wage level and people's willingness to search for a job.

Employers have their viewpoints, and the employees can have others. Employers will prefer a high degree of both security to have a job, and if not having a job then having a high level of economic security. They will further want to have good working conditions.

The balance between employers' and employees' wishes depends partly on the strength of the labour market partners, but also on the political preferences, as rules in these areas are often a combination of what the partners agree upon and the preferences at the central state level.

Recent years have seen a development with less job protection. For example, for different countries, see the OECD Indicators of Employment Protection, (www.oecd.org/els/emp/oecdindicatorsofemploymentprotection.htm), accessed 1st May, 2017.

There has also been a tendency to weaken the level of benefits (the replacement rate) based upon an argument that people will mainly search for a job if they have an economic incentive to do so, despite the fact that social contact and self-esteem also influence people's search behaviour (Fossati, 2017), further despite the fact that losing one's job has a negative impact on well-being (Eichorn, 2014). It also builds upon a view that it is mainly the economy that drives the individual, despite the fact that people are also seen as being social animals (Brooks, 2011).

## 6.6. THE IMPACT OF FREE MOVEMENT OF WORKERS AND MIGRATION

Supply and demand for labour is not only important on local, regional or national labour markets. It has increasingly become global or at least with larger geographical areas across national borders. In Europe, the free movement of workers, which was one of the fundamental pillars when the EU was set up by the Treaty of Rome in 1957, gives the right to move around and work in other countries in the EU.

Historically, the free movement of workers was used only to a more limited extent, as people tended to stay in their own country. This is because being a migrant with a lack of knowledge of language, culture and perhaps also recognition of qualifications makes it difficult to move around. However, with the gradual enlargement of the EU in this century to include Eastern Europe, there has been an increase in the number of people moving around.

The economic argument for free movement is that it will reduce unemployment as the unemployed will move to areas where there are better options for getting a job. Further, that if economic convergence takes place in the member states of the EU, then the movement will gradually be reduced due to smaller differences in earnings, but still so that the more specialised workforce will be able to move around.

However, free movement has also raised the discussion of whether some people are willing to work for a lower wage level and thereby undermine national workers – so called social dumping. It has been argued that is the case if they are willing to work for a lower wage level than national workers, and also if they are able to get welfare benefits they cannot get at home; see also Section 4.3 on welfare chauvinism. The pressure on the unskilled labour market especially, thereby increasing the risk of dualisation and a split between insiders and outsiders at the labour market, has increased the debate on migrant workers' position in different societies. This is despite the fact that, in principle, free movement overall should imply better options and possibilities at the societal level; however, these gains are not felt by those at risk of losing their job as a consequence of free movement.

## 6.7. SUMMING UP

The labour market is central to everyday life for many people, as it gives income, social contact and a feeling of purpose. Therefore, getting and keeping a job as long as one has the abilities to do so is important also for the overall development of the societies. It is central for society as production (public as well as private) takes places with labour, and increasingly the use of technology. Still, there is not just one labour market. Labour markets are divided internationally, nationally, regionally and locally, but also on the structural composition and levels of skills in each country.

We see that some have precarious jobs, some have stable and good jobs, while others are more at the outside of the labour market with many unemployment periods. The labour market thus also divides societies. Migrant workers more often have jobs with low wages and below their skill levels than people from the country they migrate to. The free movement is further looked upon by some on the labour market as a threat for their options (job and level of wage), while for others it opens opportunities. Therefore, the impact of free movement, even if neutral on societal basis, might have strong impact on some groups, while not others. In some countries unemployment among young people is high, and they seem to have been most hit by the financial crisis.

There is still in most countries a gender divide on the labour market. Women more often work part time than men, and also often have an on average lower wage, and lower level of participation rate on the labour market, whereas the level of unemployment often is the same for men and women.

People with disabilities often have difficulties in both entering and staying on the labour market, and they are therefore often having a lower participation rate.

These many differences imply therefore we need to know how the labour markets look, how they develop over the business cycle, and even more importantly, how we can expect them to develop in the years to come. This is because technological development happens very fast and will dramatically change the labour market as we now know it. The implication of this is that challenges will be increasing not decreasing in the years to come. This can imply an even more dualised labour market, and with a growing number in what has been labelled the precariat. Given the possible development central concepts such as core and periphery on the labour market can be more important to be aware of in the years to come.

The combination of flexibility and security on the labour market has large variations across countries; however, the development has tended to imply increase in flexibility and reduction in economic security, and often also in job security. Thus despite that flexicurity thus for some time has been a buzzword the combination seemingly has moved in a direction where one can question whether this in fact includes security, but mainly is flexibility.

The relationship between the state and the market is important in the field of labour market policy, as this can influence who has and who does not have access to the labour market – including the policies that might be used to change this. Chapter 7 focuses in more detail on labour market policy.

## REFERENCES

Autor, D., Levy, F. and Murnane, R. (2003), The Skill Content of Recent Technological Change: An Empirical Exploration. *Quarterly Journal of Economics*, November, pp. 1279–1333.

Brochman, G. and Dølvik, J. (2018), The Welfare State and International Migration: The European Challenge in Greve, B. ed., *The Routledge Handbook of the Welfare State*, 2nd edition. Oxon, Routledge.

Brooks, D. (2011), *The Social Animal: The Hidden Sources of Love, Character and Achievements*. New York, Random House.

Chung, H. (2016), Dualization and Subjective Employment Insecurity: Explaining the Subjective Employment Insecurity Divide Between Permanent and Temporary Workers Across 23 European Countries. *Economic and Industrial Democracy*, pp. 1–30. doi: 10.1177/0143831.X.6656411.

Doeringer, P. and Piore, M. (1971), *Internal Labor Markets and Manpower Analysis*. Lexington: Health Lexington.

Ebbinghaus, B and Manow, P. (eds.) (2001), *Comparing Welfare Capitalism Social Policy and Political Economy in Europe, Japan and the USA*. London and New York: Routledge.

Eichorn, J. (2014), The (Non-) Effect of Unemployment Benefits: Variations in the Effect of Unemployment on Life-Satisfaction Between EU Countries. *Social Indicator Research*, vol. 119, pp. 389–404.

Emmenegger, P. et al. (2012), *The Age of Dualization. The Changing Face of Inequality in Deindustrializing Societies*. Oxford, Oxford University Press.

Eurofound (2016), *What Do Europeans Do at Work? A Task-Based Analysis: European Jobs Monitor, 2016*. Luxembourg, Publications Office of the European Office.

Fossati, F. (2017), Who Wants Demanding Active Labour Market Policies? Public Attitudes Towards Policies That Put Pressure on the Unemployed. *Journal of Social Policy*, pp. 1–23. doi: 10.1017/S0047279417000216.

Friedland, D. and Price, R. (2003), Underemployment: Consequences for the Health and Well-Being of Workers. *American Journal of Community Psychology*, vol. 32, no. 1/2, pp. 33–45.

Goos, M., Manning, A. and Salomons, A. (2014), Explaining Job Polarization: Routine-Based Technological Change and Offshoring. *American Economic Review*, vol. 104, no. 8, pp. 2509–2526.

Greve, B. (2017a), *Technology and the Future of Work. The Impact on Labour Markets and Welfare States*. Cheltenham, Edward Elgar.

Greve, B. (2017b), Welfare States and Labour Market Change: What Is the Possible Relation? *Social Policy & Administration*, vol. 51, no. 2, pp. 389–403.

Greve, B. ed. (2018), *The Routledge Handbook of the Welfare State*, 2nd edition. Oxon, Routledge.

Kaplan, J. (2015), *Humans Need Not Apply. A Guide to Wealth and Work in the Age of Artificial Intelligence*. London, Yale University Press.

Lindbeck, A. and Snower, D. (1986), Wage Setting, Unemployment, and Insider-Outsider Relations. *American Economic Review*, vol. 76, no. 2, pp. 235–239.

Morel, N. (2015), Servants for the Knowledge-Based Economy? The Political Economy of Domestic Services in Europe. *Social Politics*, vol. 22, no. 2, pp. 170–192.

OECD. (2016), *Employment Outlook, 2016*. Paris, OECD Publishing.

Pearson, T. (2015), *The End of Jobs: Money, Meaning and Freedom without the 9-to-5*. New South Wales, Lioncrest.

Pfeiffer, S. (2016), Robots, Industry 4.0 and Humans, or Why Assembly Work is More than Routine Work. *Societies*, vol. 6, no. 16, pp. 1–26.

Rutledge, M. and Guan, Q. (2015), *Job Polarization and Labour Market Outcomes for Older, Middle-Skilled Workers*. CRR WP 2015–23, Boston, Center for Retirement Research.

Sage, D. (2017), Reversing the Negative Experience of Unemployment: A Mediating Role for Social Policies? *Social Policy & Administration*, pre-publication.

Seeleib-Kaiser, M. (2013), Welfare Systems in Europe and the United States. Conservative Germany Converging Toward the Liberal US Model? *International Journal of Social Quality*, vol. 3, no. 2, pp. 60–77.

Seeleib-Kaiser, M. (2016), The End of the Conservative German Welfare State Model. *Social Policy & Administration*, vol. 50, no. 2, pp. 219–240.

Spasova, S., Bouget, D., Ghailani, D. and Vanhercke, B. (2017). *Access to Social Protection for People Working on Non-Standard Contracts and as Self-Employed in Europe. A Study of National Policies*. European Social Policy Network (ESPN), Brussels: European Commission.

Standing, G. (2011), *The New Dangerous Class*. London, Bloomsbury.

Standing, G. (2014), *A Precariat Charter: From Denizens to Citizens*. London, Bloomsbury.

Tros, F. and Wilthagen, T. (2013), Flexicurity: Concepts, Practices and Outcomes in Greve, B. ed., *The Routledge Handbook of the Welfare State*. Oxon, Routledge.

# ACTIVE LABOUR MARKET POLICY

## 7.1. INTRODUCTION

Since the 1950s in Sweden there has been a long tradition of active labour market policy (ALMP) – and also in the other Nordic welfare states in Europe, but in many other countries as well; albeit as the chapter will show, the types have changed and the emphasis on ALMP as well.

The first issue to consider is what, in fact, is ALMP? In Section 7.2, the focus is on rationales and logics behind ALMP, including the understanding hereof in different countries. From this more abstract understanding of the concepts, Section 7.3 moves on to discuss the development from a focus on social inclusion, upskilling to types of activation with a work-first approach and coercion of the unemployed. The reasons why this happened are shown. The issue of life-long learning is also included. Section 7.4 highlights and presents the knowledge of what does and does not work in the ALMP. Here, as with social policy, there has increasingly been a focus on the question: Do we get value for money? This in relation to the way activation is done and whether some initiatives are better than others, and also how best to support people in their effort to be in, or reintegrated into, the labour market. Section 7.5 probes into the balance between work and family life, not often portrayed as ALMP; however, this can influence labour supply as well as the well-being of people. Last, Section 7.6 sums up the chapter.

Labour market policy often distinguishes between active and passive labour market policy. Passive labour market policy in the form of unemployment and early retirement benefit is presented in the flexicurity section in Chapter 6 (Section 6.5). Early retirement benefit is also a passive measure. However, here the choice is to focus on ALMP, as this is central in policies related to the labour market. Besides active and passive labour market policy, there are different types of regulation of the labour market, related to safety in the workplace, working times, child labour, etc., which are not covered here.

## 7.2. WHAT IS ACTIVE LABOUR MARKET POLICY?

The overall aim of ALMP is to bring people back to or into the labour market and, possibly, in times of lack of jobs to try to help people maintain the skills they have or increase them in line with future possible job openings in the labour market. Thus, ALMP also has an aim of supporting companies in having access to the people with the right qualifications for different types of jobs.

The OECD describes it in the following way:

> The objective of an effective activation policy for jobseekers and other disadvantaged groups of the population is to **bring more people into the labour force and into jobs.** This requires in particular:
>
> • ensuring that people have the **motivation and incentives** to seek employment
> • increasing their **employability** and helping them to find suitable employment
> • expanding **employment opportunities** for jobseekers and people outside the labour force
> • managing the implementation of activation policy through efficient **labour market institutions**.[1]

A central issue is, thus, that the motivation for the individual is in place, including using the right incentives to search for a job, which has been the focus in most countries' labour market policy; see also Chapter 6 on unemployment benefits. However, it is not only economic incentives for persons to actively search for a job that are important, as one might also have other incentives to do so (see later Section 7.4). Also, if a person does not have the right qualifications, it might be difficult to get a job, so ensuring people have the right qualifications is important, including human capital.

A way to depict the possible types of ALMP is to look at the statistics. Eurostat has the following information:

- **LMP services** cover all services and activities of the Public Employment Services (PES) together with any other publicly funded services for jobseekers.

  1. Labour market services

- **LMP measures** cover interventions that provide temporary support for groups that are disadvantaged in the labour market and which aim at activating the unemployed, helping people move from involuntary inactivity into employment, or maintaining the jobs of persons threatened by unemployment. . . .

  2. Training
  3. (Not used anymore – included in category 4)
  4. Employment incentives
  5. Supported employment and rehabilitation
  6. Direct job creation
  7. Start-up incentives[2]

The services available to the unemployed (and companies) are the public employment services (PES), which can work alone or together with other services for jobseekers. They have varied roles in different countries, but they often act as a link between the unemployed and the companies, and they often also help the unemployed in searching for a job, how to write an application, etc. Depending on the unemployment insurance system, the PES might also have the role of controlling that the unemployed are actively searching for a job. For companies, it can be a place to ask whether there are people with specific qualifications who are actually searching for a job and might be referred to work for the company. The PES are increasingly supported by electronic systems monitoring the activities and informing about the situation for the unemployed and on the labour market more specifically, including local and regional differences.

The measures, used by the PES and/or other actors, range from different kinds of education (no. 2: training) to incentives by supporting employers by wage-subsidies, practical work in companies (no. 4: employment incentives), to rehabilitation and support for different types of jobs for people in early retirement benefit (no. 5: supported employment and rehabilitation) to direct job creation (no. 6), and various incentives to start up a private company and, as a consequence, be self-employed (no. 7: start-up incentives). Training and employment incentives are the types which are mainly used. There is a higher spending in the Nordic countries, lower in central Europe and very low in Southern and Eastern Europe – albeit with national differences.

The way in which the EU and the OECD describe ALMP thus points to the fact that a number of issues are important for a successful ALMP. This includes, as shown in Figure 7.1 motivation, opportunities and employability. If these aspects are important, then it is also important to focus on policy measures that can help in achieving and supporting these aspects in ALMP

Figure 7.1 is, further, a clear reminder that if one wants to support the labour market (companies as well as individual persons) to better be able to match demand and supply of labour it is important to look into motivation (the incentives), but also whether people do, in fact, have the necessary qualifications so that they are employable and continue to be employable. The ladder in the figure (labelled "opportunities") also informs about the fact that some might be a long distance away from getting a job, while others have already taken the first steps onto the labour market and might be on the way to the next and perhaps better job. It also reinforces the knowledge that the overall demand for labour is important for the ability to get a job. The interaction between institutions and policies thereby is also important.

A further issue is how to reduce the possible discrimination on the labour market, for example, the risk that certain groups might have more difficulties than others to enter or re-enter the labour market. Discrimination is difficult to combat as it is, as a

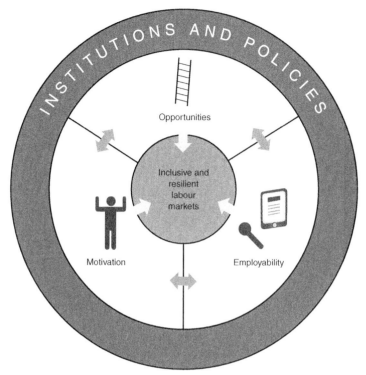

*Figure 7.1*    Key elements for successful activation strategies
Source: OECD, 2015, p. 109

rule—not open discrimination, but hidden and indirect in the way the employment process functions. So, part of ALMP can also be to have a focus on how to counteract discrimination, which can include affirmative action, but also, for example, to give support at the workplace to people with disabilities, including special aids and equipment (help-remedies), making it possible for them to do the job.

## 7.3. DIFFERENT AIMS OF ACTIVE LABOUR MARKET POLICY

Different aims of ALMP can be depicted – and this varies across different countries, partly for ideological differences and partly for historical reasons. Therefore, the concept of ALMP can have different understandings and support in different nations. The Nordic countries were the first to embrace ALMP, and are still high spenders from the state purse in pursuing ALMP. Overall, the aim being that especially in recession times with often higher levels of unemployment (as after the last fiscal crisis), people could be trained or have different kinds of work experience, making it possible for them to enter or re-enter the labour market in better times when demand for labour is again increasing. Therefore, periods of unemployment were used as part of the explanation for the development of ALMP.

ALMP with the aim of increasing employment by stimulating demand has, for a long time, been a possible instrument. This can include higher public sector spending, and lowering of taxes and duties, but also direct construction of new infrastructure can in times of recession be used to create jobs. Whether or not ALMP is used depends greatly on the influence of ideas and whether one believes in supply side or demand side types of interventions.

Table 7.1 shows the aims and tools related to different kinds of ALMP.

The fact that there are a variety of types of ALMP also reflects the different ideas and aims of the policy; see also Chapter 5 on ideas in social policy.

*Table 7.1*  Four types of active labour market policy

|  | Investment in human capital | | |
|---|---|---|---|
| Pro-market employment orientation | None | Weak | Strong |
| Weak | Passive benefits | Occupation: job-creation schemes in the public sector. Non-employment-related training programmes | Basic education |
| Strong | Incentive reinforcement: tax credits, in work benefits. Time limits on recipiency, benefit reductions, benefit conditionality | Employment assistance: placement services, job subsidies, counselling, job-search programmes | Upskilling: job-related vocational training |

Source: Bonoli (2010, p. 441)

The incentive reinforcement which is a strong pro-market approach to ALMP without the emphasis on investment in human capital has, as its central idea, that if the economic incentives are high enough (building on *homo economicus*, for example that people are rational, individual, utility-maximising individuals), then they will find a job as they will also be willing to take a job at a low level of wage. Further, they will take any kind of job as long as it is a job. Tax credits and in-work benefits work as these are available only when one has a job, and thereby those who are unemployed will have a lower disposable income. This is on the positive incentive side of taking a job, whereas the negative approach includes restrictions on, and sanctions, etc. related to unemployment benefit because people who do not get a job will have no or only limited support from the welfare state. Thereby, there is a connection between social and labour market policies and the choice of access to and levels of social policy benefits. The other types of ALMP have this connection to a lesser degree as they focus more on finding different pathways back to the labour market by using support to get a job, increasing the level of education ranging from basic education to upskilling and improvement of skills in order to match the actual demand on the labour market.

The approaches in Table 7.1 involve different degrees of coerciveness and voluntary aspects. This will depend on the specific national system of labour market policy and also to what degree the focus is on improving human capital; see also Dean's typology on the welfare-to-work nexus, later.

Employment assistance has a focus on the fact that there can be obstacles for a person to get a job. For some, this can be lack of knowledge on how to write an application, how to search for a job; other unemployed might need a subsidy to reduce the employer's cost for a time until their productivity has increased. This is especially important for the long-term unemployed, as they might need experience in working on the labour market and employers might argue that they are not willing to pay the going wage rate for those persons. Long-term unemployment signals to employers that a person perhaps lacks different types of qualifications (which will differ from sector to sector).

Another activity is to ask unemployed people to do some work in return for the benefit they receive – typically in the public sector. Again, this might have a coercive nature, but it can also be inclusive in its focus, as continuing to work in a job might reduce the risk of reduction of the human capital acquired by the person.

Last, education has been a central issue in several types of ALMPs. Thus, investment in human capital by different kinds of education and/or vocational training can help a person into or already on the labour market. Here we also have an example of what can be labelled "social investment". Ensuring that all have a central basic education makes it more possible for people to be able to work and also participate in continuously upskilling and re-skilling. This can be understood as an investment in people's human capital so that it is sufficiently high in order to be able to re- or integrate them onto the labour market.

The difference in approach to ALMP, including the focus on workfare, can be depicted in the following way:

a) Human-capital development (egalitarian and competitive is the focus)
b) Coercive (work first, where authoritarian and competitive is the focus)
c) Active job-creating (egalitarian and inclusion is the focus)
d) Insertion/right to work (authoritarian and inclusive is the focus)
(based upon Dean, 2007)

This implies that countries having an ALMP might have it for different reasons, and it might also change over times. In most countries, recent years have seen a stronger focus on work first, thus also sometimes labelled a move from welfare to workfare (Bryson, 2003). This also raises the question: Who is supporting the different types of ALMP? It can be argued that there is a broader support for the ALMP that focuses on human-capital development and active job creation (*a* plus *c* in Dean's understanding) and less on the more coercive matters, thus also raising the question: Who wants demanding labour market policies (Fossati, 2017)? Fossati also argues that many workfare activities are implemented despite the fact that those who should benefit from them do not necessarily find that they do.

The focus in the ALMP to a larger degree has been on the supply side, and less on the demand side. This, in combination with workfare approaches, has also implied that the spending on ALMP in many countries is rather low.

Life-long learning, which has been seen gradually as important in order to continue to be able to get and/or keep a job, is differently developed in many countries, and here companies might play a larger role than in the more traditional ALMP where the states have often had the central role.

The variation in approach is also a reason why the approach to, and the understanding of, flexicurity can vary between countries; see also Chapter 6.

## 7.4. WHAT DOES AND DOES NOT WORK IN ACTIVE LABOUR MARKET POLICY?

Many instruments have been, and will be, used in ALMP; see also the presentation in Section 7.2 of the many and possible varieties in activations. A central question is: What does and does not work? There is now a lot of knowledge hereabout, mainly in the short-run, but also issues related to long-time perspectives and consequences of activation (Nordlund and Greve, 2018).

There are several reasons for the need to know what does and does not work. These include:

a) To ensure the best use of scarce economic resources
b) To best help people back to the labour market
c) To avoid possible bottlenecks
d) To ensure the best incentives

Many studies exist (see, for example, Calmfors, 1994; Martin and Grubb, 2001; Martin, 2014; Card, Kluve and Weber, 2015; Caliendo and Schmidl, 2016), including those that generalize numerous studies of activation. Studies in ALMP cover different age groups, levels of education, occupational sectors, geographic entities in different countries, different business cycles and a variety of welfare states with different passive benefit systems (unemployment and early retirement benefit).

A central aspect of evaluating what works and for whom is, besides the impact of the business cycle, what would have happened anyhow (deadweight loss). This refers to how many of those unemployed activated would have gotten a job by themselves without any intervention. If they could have done this, then spending money on the initiative has not, in itself, changed the position of the persons on the labour market.

Another issue is whether – and this is especially the case with wage support to companies – due to subsidies, employers shift from a person employed without a subsidy to a person with a subsidy, because if this is the case then there will be no net effect of the activation.

Overall, across countries and different sizes of ALMP, it seems that what works is mainly activation in private companies, and increasing human capital by investing in training and education during times of economic recession. This is in contrast to activation in the public sector, which does not seem to increase the likelihood of entry or re-entry to the labour market, and might even have a negative impact (Caliendo and Schmidl, 2016). The authors also point to the fact that job-search assistance might be positive for young people. So, to sum-up, the impact of ALMP seems to confirm that the most effective intervention is activation in the private sector both in the short and long run, followed by training and retraining programmes (Vooren, Haelermans, Groot and Brink, 2016). The authors also point to the fact that PES might even have a negative impact on employment. A possible reason for the lack of effectiveness in public sector employment can be that there are fewer job openings, and the public sector is often the one obliged to do the activation if there is no option in the private sector.

Education and training are often not only issues for the state but also for companies that want to keep their workforce up to date, and they might also be included in occupational agreements and agreements on the individual workplace.

Although it is not always possible to show the impact, some would argue that the existence of work-activation in itself increases the likelihood that some more actively search for a job themselves

This is because they will otherwise have to participate in activation which they suspect might not lead them towards the labour market and might not even be very attractive.

Whereas studies on the impact of specific types of activation give some information, it is less clear how economic incentives influence the way back to the labour market, including how different kinds of in-work credits have an impact.

Furthermore, it might be difficult to transform policy from one country to another as the economic situation is different in individual countries, as are the qualifications of the workforce and the structure of the societies. Still, information on what works can provide further insight and can be used as ideas of how to pursue labour market policy in other countries.

ALMP can thus be important if done in the best way, and not only as a means to force people back to the labour market.

## 7.5. WORK–FAMILY LIFE BALANCE

The balance between work and family life is not ordinarily seen as part of ALMP. However, one can argue that ensuring the balance between work and family will make people happier, more productive and often provide a better life for children. Presumably, the reason for not including the work–family life balance in ALMP is that this is not only a role for the state, but also for employers, albeit there is often a connection between what the state does and what companies do. Even civil society might have a role; for example, grandparents might help in taking care of grandchildren and thus enable both parents, if they wish, to have a job. Albeit, in many countries, the support from grandparents has, in reality, been reduced in recent years because both men and women are on the labour market, and stay there longer than previously.

The state's role in supporting the work–family life balance is often related to two sets of policies.

One is leave systems. Leave (maternity/paternity) can support the balance between work and family life, although the impact depends on the size of the income transfer related to taking leave. The length of the leave also influences the balance for families with newborn children. However, a too-long leave might have a negative repercussion, especially for women, on job security and their lifetime income, as employers might be scared by the risk of employing a person who will be away from work for a long time shortly after being taken on. The impact also depends on how companies support leave. Information on the different leave systems can be found on the website of the International Network on Leave Policies & Research.[3]

The other role for the state relates to whether or not there is affordable and high-quality day care because, if this is the case, it supports people's ability both to work and to have a family life. With increasing life expectancy, not only day care for children can be important, but also long-term care for the elderly can be a factor helping the reconciliation of work and family life.

Companies might support it by having flexibility for the workers so that they can work at times when it fits with the rest of the family, by being able to take a day off if a child is sick, or leaving the workplace if a member of the family needs support. So, a high degree of flexibility can be an important issue in the way for people to both work and have a family life.

## 7.6. SUMMING UP – THE WAY FORWARD FOR LABOUR MARKET POLICY

The labour market policy is now a central policy area in many welfare states. A core reason for this is that in the wake of the financial crisis, and even before, in many countries there have been high levels of unemployment, with many, including young people, trying to enter the labour market. High levels of unemployment imply a risk of stronger inequalities and more split societies.

ALMP can have many varied types of approaches. This is due to that there will be different emphases on the core focus of the policy ranging from a work-first to a human-capital development approach, depending on the different sizes and state economic involvement. Upgrading and improving of human capital is seen as a central issue in the coming years. The focus in some countries is not on ALMP, but instead on letting the market work, and this often with the expectation that people will take up the job available often without any need for active support from the welfare state – people, it is argued, can get jobs if they are willing to reduce their wage demands.

The social security is also different. This is due to that the generosity of unemployment benefit varies across countries, and sometimes the size of the unemployment benefits is used as an argument for the job-search intensity among the unemployed.

Although the labour market policy here has had a central focus on the role of the state, in many countries, the labour market partners are central as a way of ensuring a stable labour market, upskilling the workforce and the creation of new jobs. This is also as the partners agree upon wages and working conditions through the collective agreements.

The labour market is also of central importance for many individuals, as it gives an income and access to social relations, and thus unemployment can have a negative impact on the well-being of people. In fact, it is evident that being in risk of becoming unemployed has a highly negative impact on well-being, and unemployment benefit is further not able to get people back to the level of well-being they had before becoming unemployed. A new job will be the best way to increase well-being.

Family life is also of central importance for many people, so that policies that support this combination also have an impact on the way the labour market functions, and making it possible for people to keep their job when becoming a parent can thus also be argued to be a kind of ALMP. The work–family life balance can thereby also be considered as part of the active labour market policy.

The chapter has further discussed what works and what does not work in active labour market policy. It seems that ALMP will mainly work if activation takes place in private companies, as there often might be better job opportunities here, but also education and human-capital improvement might work in times of recession, making it possible for people take up jobs in new areas or when demand of labour is back.

For welfare states, labour markets are also important, as those who are earning their own money do not need financial support from the welfare state. It ensures income to the welfare state as people with income pay income tax, VAT, etc. Thus, the sustainability of the welfare state is also influenced by the way in which the labour market works.

## NOTES

1 www.oecd.org/employment/activation.htm, accessed 24th March, 2017; emphasis in original.
2 http://ec.europa.eu/eurostat/cache/metadata/en/lmp_esms.htm, accessed 24th March, 2017
3 www.leavenetwork.org/.

## REFERENCES

Bonoli, G. (2010), The Political Economy of Active Labor-Market Policy. *Politics & Society*, vol. 38, no. 4, pp. 435–457. doi: 10.1177/0032329210381235.

Bryson, A. (2003), *From Welfare to Workfare* in J. Millar ed., *Understanding Social Security: Issues for Policy and Practice*. Bristol, Policy Press.

Caliendo, M. and Schmidl, R. (2016), Youth Unemployment and Active Labor Market Policies in Europe. *IZA Journal of Labor Policy*, vol. 5, no. 1, pp. 1–30.

Calmfors, L. (1994), Active Labour Market Policy and Unemployment – A Framework for the Analysis of Crucial Design Features, OECD Economic Studies No. 22. Paris, OECD.

Card, D., Kluve, J. and Weber, A. (2015), What Works? A Meta Analysis of Recent Active Labor Market Program Evaluations, NBER Working Paper No. 21431. Cambridge, NBER.

Dean, H. (2007), The Ethics of Welfare-to-Work. *Policy & Politics*, vol. 35, no. 4, pp. 573–589.

Fossati, F. (2017), Who Wants Demanding Active Labour Market Policies? Public Attitudes towards Policies That Put Pressure on the Unemployed. *Journal of Social Policy*, pp. 1–23. doi: 10.1017/S0047279417000216.

Martin, J. (2014), Activation and Active Labour Market Policies in OECD Countries: Stylized Facts and Evidence on Their Effectiveness. IZA Policy Paper No. 84, Bonn, IZA.

Martin, J. and Grubb, D. (2001), What Works and for Whom: A Review of OECD Countries' Experiences with Active Labour Market Policies, Working Paper, Institute for Labour Market Policy Evaluation, No. 14. Uppsala, IFAU.

Nordlund, M. and Greve, B. (2018), Active Labour Market Policies in Greve, B. ed., *The Routledge Handbook of the Welfare State*, 2nd edition. Oxon, Routledge.

OECD. (2015), *Employment Outlook, 2015*. Paris, OECD.

Vooren, M., Haelermans, C., Groot, W. and Brink, H. (2016), *The Effectiveness of Active Labour Market Policies: A Systematic Meta-Analysis*. www.sole-jole.org/17403.pdf, 14th of June, 2017.

# THE FUTURE

## 8.1. INTRODUCTION

The focus in this book is on describing, analysing and presenting central aspects of social and labour market policy with a view to how this can be understood in the light of history, ideas, and economic and political development. This also includes the ability to finance expenditures and the legitimacy of the chosen policies.

This last chapter has a more explorative focus on the possible future development of social and labour market policy. Considering the future will always be more speculative, despite historical tendencies to follow a path. This, as the path can be deviating, can be changed due to new options available, or in ideologies. Despite the difficulties in predicting the future, one might be able to look into what the possible challenges are, and with the knowledge and analytical framework we have today, how we can determine what the possible changes will be.

Before looking into the future challenges, Section 8.2 briefly argues why social and labour market policy has been and is still important – for societies and for individuals. After a discussion of future challenges, the chapter sums up the central messages of the book.

## 8.2. WHY IS SOCIAL AND LABOUR MARKET POLICY IMPORTANT?

Labour market and social policy is important for individuals, the state and the market. This is the case for a number of different reasons.

In simple terms, social and labour market policy is imperative as, in a variety of ways, it supports the individual with:

a) services – for example, hospital in case of sickness
b) benefits – for example, social assistance when in economic need

Some welfare states have a higher focus on benefits, whereas in others there is also a stronger development towards delivery and financing of more services. As an example of an area with large differences among countries is long-term care systems, especially for the elderly. In the Northern part of Europe this is highly developed and important as a state welfare, whereas in other countries this is less developed, and to a higher degree something that the civil society (mainly family and relatives) are expected to do by delivering help to those frail elderly (Greve, 2017a). Delivery of services can influence not only the daily life of those in possible need of service, but can also be important for the labour market. This is the case if lack of service implies that people do not enter and/or leave the labour market in order to do care work in the family. This is not only an issue within the field of long-term care, but also day care for children.

Historically, day care for children was mainly an issue for the families where the mother stayed at home and took care of the children, whereas the man was on the labour market. Therefore things were often framed as the male-breadwinner system. However, with the development of day care for children it was possible for both men and women to stay on the labour market. It might even have a negative impact on fertility rate if there is a lack of day care, and this, for some, can imply that they do not want to have children, as they then cannot participate on the labour market. This can on the European level be witnessed by the low fertility rate and also that a central recommendation from the European Union is to have high-quality day care at affordable prices.

Having high-quality day care can thus be seen as supporting labour market participation for both men and women, but can also be argued to be a social investment. This is the case if a high quality of care supports children's development, as this might reduce welfare expenditure in other areas (Heckman, 2006).

Thus, the many and varied types of services and benefits ensures, to different degrees in various countries, that people can have a good life. The degree of decommodification (for example, the ability to live a life without working on the labour market), also varies across countries, and the same is the case in relation to how dependent persons are on having a family, both for economic and caring reasons.

The impact of the policies on equality and poverty is also different between different countries. This partly reflects the fact that the generosity of benefits and progressivity of the tax system varies among countries. Some countries have, for example, a progressive income tax system, whereas others have flat-rate systems. Welfare states have, if they wish to, the option to ensure redistribution between rich and poor, but also helping in economic transfer over the whole life perspective.

Naturally, social and labour market policy does not work without being in contact with other parts of societies. Thus, for example, the labour market policy's ability to integrate or reintegrate to the labour market is highly dependent on the educational system and the human and social capital individuals have. Still, ALMP that can then further increase and develop human capital by training and further educating has an important role to ensure employability, but also because, for many, having a job is an important aspect of life and well-being.

For society, social and labour market policy can help reduce those of need of economic support from the state by having ensured a qualified labour supply. Social policy can, by for example, caring for children and the frail elderly, also cause a social investment so that both men and women can be on the labour market, and also so that investment in children by means of good day care increases the likelihood of them growing up and being socially integrated into society. At the same time, paying out benefits helps reduce the cyclical impact of the economic development because in-cash benefits often work as automatic stabilisers in societies. Thus, social and labour market policy not only helps the individual, but is also an instrument for ensuring a stable economic and political development.

For the market, social and labour market policy can help in safeguarding that the labour force has the necessary qualifications so that companies' competitiveness is high, and also that there is buying power for goods and services even in times of low economic activity, for example, the automatic stabilisers by income transfers. At the same time, in most countries the state buys a lot of goods and services from the market in order to deliver services (this can be in day-care institutions, hospitals, long-term care and education). So, the market and, as a consequence, many companies are highly dependent on having a state with demand for their goods and services.

A possible conflict is the impact of how to finance the welfare state, as this also requires taxes and duties, where some of them might have an impact on the balance between work and leisure, and also saving and consumption.

In all countries there further will be persons who either are born with a disability, or due to sickness and/or accident will have a disability. These persons will be in need of different kinds of income transfers and/or service in order to have lives as close as possible to others.

Thus, there is, and will presumably always be, a challenge of finding the best balance between these issues. Still, there are future challenges, which is the focus of Section 8.3.

## 8.3.  FUTURE CHALLENGES FOR SOCIAL AND LABOUR MARKET POLICY

Future challenges refer especially to the ability to finance social and labour market policy. They further revolve around a number of topics, some which have been in existence for some time, and others which have come more into the debate in the wake of the financial crisis starting in 2008/09.

The ageing of the population has, for some time, been a worry in many European countries, as well as in countries such as Japan and China. The ageing of populations, so the argument goes, increases the need for economic support in cash (pensions), as well as more services in relation to health and long-term care. This while, at the same time, there are relatively fewer people on the labour market and thereby paying taxes to the state. If fewer people pay tax, this might reduce the option to finance the welfare state.

In several countries, this has already led to pension reforms – causing an increase in the pensionable age, as well as changing the formulas for how to calculate pensions. This includes moving from a pay-as-you-go system to a funded pension system, where the pension depends on what has been, in one way or another, paid into a pension fund and/or how many years one has been on the labour market. This has been done in order to reduce the financial pressure on welfare states, while at the same time it has an inbuilt risk of increasing inequality in the living standards of the elderly. Thus those who have been more or less permanently on the labour market (the insiders, core) will have a higher level of pension than those with less strong attachment to the labour market (the outsiders, periphery). Inequality in working age might thus continue in the pension age implying different quality of life for the elderly.

It has also been argued that the growing number of elderly could cause a lack of manpower; however, in most countries, the unemployment rates are relatively high, also for young people, so this does not in itself seem to be a core issue and impact of the change in demography. Furthermore, it seems that the elderly's being in better health today than earlier implies that they stay longer on the labour market. This is witnessed by the average age of retirement going up as well as the number of years people are on the labour market. The last issue albeit slightly reduced in that more young people today take a longer education than previously.

Higher average life expectancy is also having an impact on the number of elderly and thereby pension expenditures (the size dependent on the specific pension system), although the many reforms of the size and stronger focus on occupational pension already has reduced this pressure. Whether there is increased cost to health care and long-term care is a more open question. This is because, as also indicated previously, not only are people living longer, but they are also often healthier than they were before, and thus the need for support and health care might not necessarily increase because of the higher numbers of elderly persons. Part of this also reflects development in the use of rehabilitation, re-enablement and welfare technology (Greve, 2017a); rehabilitation, for example, makes it possible for people to stay longer in their own homes and be better able to take care of themselves. At the same time, many elderly may prefer to live where they have lived for many years.

New technology might (as argued in Chapters 6 and 7) have a strong impact on the labour market, and as argued previously, the use of new welfare technology might also reduce economic pressure on the welfare state in relation to long-term care, but also in relation to health care. As shown by Frey and Osborne (2013), there is a high risk that up to, and in some countries over, 50% of the job functions existing today will not exist in 10–15 years' time. Naturally, there will also be new jobs; however, it looks as though there will be fewer jobs in the future, and the implications on the way in which to enact, finance and structure social and labour market policy are still not clear.

To give just one example, the use of new platforms to buy and sell goods as part of the new technology can also have profound impact on societies (Greve, 2017b), as the boundaries between employed and self-employed become blurred, and those providing work on the platforms might not be covered by collective agreements, and have no rights as they are considered to be self-employed; see, for a description, Hill (2015). Working on platform can also increase the risk of becoming working poor, e.g. even if those working have an income below the relative poverty line of 60% of median income. In recent years there has been an increase so that now around one in every ten in EU-member states are working poor. New technology, use of platforms, etc. might increase this percentage, and this can give rise to a stronger dualisation of societies. Thus, even having a job might not ensure a decent living standard. As it is the relative line used, this is related to the situation in each country. Further, it might increase the need for even more ALMP than actually is delivered today.

Migration has been a challenge for social and labour market policy for some time. This includes both migration within the EU and migration from developing countries to developed countries. This is because it touches upon normative issues on who is deserving and who is not deserving, but also in relation to types of jobs, and who can get a job. The increased polarisation on the labour market increases the risk that especially the unskilled are not able to get or find a job, and this risk will presumably increase in the years to come, the implication being that they feel that they are more threatened by migration than others, and have the feeling that migrants only come to receive welfare benefits. This fear seems to exist both related to migration in the EU and between countries outside the EU, but also between, for example, the US and Mexico. This has raised in many countries discussion on who shall have access to benefits and of what size, increasing the old debate on who deserves and who does not deserve social benefits and services.

At the same time, the technological development increases the possibility that some jobs to a greater extent than today can be done at a distance, so that people willing to work for a lower hourly wage can do so from the nation in which they live and where living costs are lower than in a possible new country, so that they do not need to physically migrate. This increases the likelihood that for some people in the more affluent countries, it will be even more difficult to compete on the labour market.

Thereby, globalisation, already seen by some as strongly negative for their position, can have an even stronger impact on the jobs and options available in different countries.

Furthermore, global development also influences and can have negative repercussions on the ability to finance welfare states – not only due to movement of jobs, but also as the use of transfer pricing and tax havens might reduce the tax paid in developed welfare states. If there are fewer taxes and duties for the state, this will cause difficulties in financing social and labour market policy. Thereby, the ability to finance welfare states in the future has come under threat, and with that a risk that social and labour market policy to a larger degree will be less developed than it is today.

This also points to the risk of losing legitimacy for social and labour market policy, as with migration mentioned previously, of the welfare state. This happens if people are afraid that those they find not to be deserving get the benefit, and that jobs are outsourced to other countries. This, while at the same time the new social risks, as discussed in Chapter 3, de facto might imply a need for more social and labour market policy also to ensure, as a central example, that the important work–family life balance is achieved.

## 8.4. POSSIBLE CHANGES

As a consequence of the depicted possible challenges, traditional policies might be more difficult to enact in the future unless re-distributional policies are part of societies' development – and that might include higher taxes on the wealthiest persons. Willingness to pay taxes and duties in order to finance social policies can thus be an issue where there also can be a conflict between different perspectives on how welfare states shall develop in the years to come dependent on the ideological stance of different actors. How this balance will be struck will vary among countries; thus also the structure and encompassing of social and labour market policy will presumably in the years to come also vary greatly. This implies also a variation in possible change. Both the depicted possible change in the scenarios later will naturally be influenced by at least a certain kind of path-dependency.

If the idea having the central impact is the neo-liberal paradigm, we will be witnessing a development where social and labour market policy will less encompassing. It will further presumably be with a very high degree of targeting of benefits so that only those most poor (and seen as deserving) will get an income transfer. There will also be a lower level of welfare service financed by the state, and, instead even more focus on that the market shall be the central provider of social policy in the future. In this scenario ALMP will also be only more limited as it instead will be the expectation that people are willing to take any job with any wage, and, if in need of training, it will be either the companies or the individual who will have to pay Occupational welfare can be an important aspect of changes in this direction. This will be a development with a high risk of increasing levels of inequality and even more segregated societies.

If the focus is more on the social-investment perspective, one can expect increased focus on initiatives such as ALMP where people will be in a better position to be able to be on the labour market. Investment in child care and long-term care of high quality can also be seen as possible issues as this will help in forming societies with stronger social cohesion. How to ensure well-being and a high level of quality of life (happiness) will be of central importance for decision makers. In this scenario, there will also be instruments used to reduce the degree of inequality, both as an ideological ambition, but also as higher degrees of equality might make it possible to ensure more coherent societies, and perhaps in some countries an even higher level of economic growth. Despite, as argued, that there will be a focus on quality of life, there will also be an interest in economic growth, as higher levels of economic growth will make it more possible to finance income transfers and delivery of social service. In this way, the state will still have a central role in the development, while not neglecting that the market can deliver part of welfare, and, that also civil society still can be an important aspect of societal development. Levels of benefits will also tend to be higher and more encompassing, again both as a way to reduce inequality, but also as way of ensuring economic demand in societies.

Globalisation and regionalisation will, in both scenarios, still play a role for social and labour market policy. Whether the free movement will be as large as it is now is open for interpretation. If the economies grow and the differences in living standards among countries, especially within the EU, are reduced, then free movement will be reduced – and this further as depicted earlier due to the use of new technologies. Still, both issues imply constant challenges for the ability to finance welfare states.

## 8.5. SUMMING UP

Social and labour market policy is central for most developed countries in order to ensure a high level of well-being and a trust in the future, including building the necessary social and human capital, which we know will make more cohesive societies. This is because many people are, over the life course, dependent on the policies. Still, many social policies often ensure a good start in life – but also provide support in later life. From the cradle to the grave is thus still a central aspect of societies' development, not only as an aspect of importance for individuals, but also as a way of making societies cohesive and well functioning. However, the pressure on health and long-term care, retrenchment in the level of certain benefits in some countries also points to a weakened position of these policies in recent years.

Retrenchment of benefits might not only have a negative impact on those receiving the benefits. Companies that want to sell goods and services need buyers, so that many people having an income to spend will be a prerequisite also for companies to survive, and therefore retrenchment might also be negative for companies, and this can then imply fewer jobs, besides the reduction as a consequence of new technology. A risk of a vicious cycle starts to develop. In this way social and labour market policy might in the years to come be even more important than they have been historically.

How specifically to enact policies will vary across countries, and some will follow their historical path, whereas others will use windows of opportunity to change the systems and the strategies they pursue. This is because ideas have an impact on development, but also as development can have various impacts on different parts of societies. The debate on welfare chauvinism is an indicator of a development in some countries where the distinction is not necessarily between the classical who deserves versus who does not deserve, but more between a "them and us".

At the same time, all countries will need to look for strategies to make the best use of the available money, and try to make the administration as simple as possible. Although this is easy to write and to have as a goal, it is difficult to implement. Evidence of what works will also be an important issue if a social-investment paradigm shall have a chance to develop. As always, there is opportunity cost, i.e. spending money on issues implies that this money can't be spent on other areas. So, even if it can be difficult to depict quality, for example, of care to children and elderly, there will be a need to be stronger informed on how best to achieve quality.

Nevertheless, there seems to be a continuously strong need for social and labour market policy, which will continue to be the case in the years to come. National preference will prevail, but also learning from each other will be central, and, finally, social and labour market policy can be prerequisite for social cohesion and the ability to cope with the possible dramatic changes on the labour market as a consequence of new technology.

## REFERENCES

Frey, C. and Osborne, M. (2013), *The Future of Employment: How Susceptible Are Jobs to Computerisation?* Oxford Department of Engineering Science, Oxford University.

Greve, B. ed. (2017a), *Long-Term Care for the Elderly in Europe: Development and Prospect.* Oxon, Routledge.

Greve, B. (2017b), *Technology and the Future of Work: The Impact on Labour Markets and Welfare States.* Cheltenham, Edward Elgar.

Heckman, J. (2006), Skill Formation and the Economics of Investing in Disadvantaged Children. *Science*, New Series, vol. 312, no. 5782, pp. 1900–1902.

Hill, S. (2015), *Raw Deal: How the "Uber Economy" and Runaway Capitalism Are Screwing American Workers.* New York, St. Martin's Press.

# INDEX

Printed in Great Britain
by Amazon